MW01233122

# Drop The Rage, Turn The Page!

A Case for Religious Freedom, Race, Religion and Politics, God and Government

## *Drop The Rage, Turn The Page!*
A Case for Religious Freedom, Race, Religion and Politics, God and Government

Copies of this book may be obtained by contacting
Dr. T. DeWitt Smith, Jr.
Hope Publishing House
1215 Tuckawanna Dr. SW
Atlanta, GA 30311

Hope Publishing House Web Page

Or
Your local Book Vendor

Biblical quotations are from the Holy Bible - King James Version (KJV), 1976 by Royal Publisher, Inc., Nashville, TN. The Holy Bible: New International Version (NIV) © Copyright 1973, 1978, 1984 by the International Bible Society. Used by permission of Zondervan Bible Publishers. All other quotation are from The Holy Bible KJV unless attributed to the New King James Version (NKJ) Copyright © 1982, by Thomas Nelson, Inc., Used by Permission ; the New American Standard Bible (NASB), © 1962, 1963, 1968, 1971, 1972, 1973, 1975, 1977, by the Lockman Foundation, Used by permission; and Today's English Version (TEV) © 1988, American Bible Society, Used by permission.

Library of Congress Control Number: 2011924015

Printed in East Point, Georgia

Other Books by T. DeWitt Smith, Jr.

*Deacon In The Black Baptist Church*, 1983, 1992 – Hope Publishing House – Atlanta, GA.

*Putting Lay(people) To Work*

*Membership Orientation Handbook*

*New Testament Deacon Ministry In African American Churches,*

*Spiritual Gifts For Godly People*

*Training Trustees For Baptist Churches*

*Deaconess On Duty*

General Editor*: Baptists Are Alive, 2004,* by Atlanta Missionary Baptist Association. Published by the AMBA Baptist Press, Atlanta GA

Contributing Writer: *Gardner C. Taylor: Submissions to the Dean,* 2009. J. Douglas Wiley and Ivan Douglas Hicks, Editors. Published by Urban Ministries, Inc: Chicago, IL., Essay and a sermon entitled "Recovering The Cutting Edge."

## Dedications and Acknowledgements

This book is dedicated to my wife Aretta who continues to inspire and pray for me; to my four children, and our thirteen grandchildren, nephews and nieces, and their children for whom life holds so much promise.

This book is also dedicated to my church family: Trinity Baptist Church of Metro Atlanta; to the Progressive National Baptist Convention where I served as 18th President, and before that, in other offices of the convention.

I am indebted to Dr. Gardner C. Taylor and former President Jimmy Carter for their insights; my nephew Ernest Benion, Jr., for his stimulating thoughts on health and faith. I must acknowledge my indebtedness to my Sister-in-law Beverly Ross. Her keen eye caught obvious mistakes that would otherwise cripple the reader's focus with having to ponder what an author means. Special thanks to Mr. & Mrs. Wallace and Peggy Mapp, and Mr. Alton Jamal Johnson, for reading this work and offering helpful corrections and suggestions.

Thanks to Dr. K. Gerone Free for permission to print his prayer and prophecy in full.

I wish to thank the following publishing companies for permission to quote.

*Race Matters*, by Cornel West
Copyright © 1993, 2001 by Cornel West
Reprinted by permission of Beacon Press, Boston

*Bible and Ethics in Christian Life*, by Bruce C. Birch and Larry Rasmussen
Copyright © 1976, Augsburg Fortress Publishers, Minneapolis, MN

*Benjamin E. May, His Life, Contributions, and Legacy*, edited by Dr. Samuel DuBois Cook. Copyright © 2009, Providence Publishing Corporation, Franklin, TN

*Eight Habits of the Heart*, by Clifton Taulbert
Copyright © 1997, Penguin Books, New York

# Table Of Contents

# Preface

I have entitled this book *Drop The Rage, Turn the Page*, as an indication that American political rhetoric and protests have found a vicious ally with hatred. It could be an explosive and untenable platform for future campaigning. This type of rage is also an attack upon religious liberty with its tentacles turned on a believing President who some have tried to paint as an unbeliever where Christianity is concerned. It seems to me that there is quite a bit of rage over President Obama being in office. There seems to be an atmosphere that bespeaks hatred for our nation's leader; something the world around us is keeping up with, watching to see if the Nation that is known to be the stronghold of democracy and fair play is suddenly running afoul of her fundamental beliefs that shape this democratic republic.

I have never in my life, personally witnessed so much negative campaigning, and talk that America must be brought back to her original founding principles. The rhetoric of rage in politics is so alive that the very adults children look up to, are giving little children a history lesson on incivility and indecency. The Tea Party signs have showed racial insensitivity in its vilest form: hatred for America's President; the attacking of black Congressmen. Government is not black government; government is people. In the United States of America, government is of the people, by the people and for the people. What are the people doing when they turn political disagreement into rage that causes hatred? This type of rage must give way to better campaigning and dealing with the issues; thus my title, *Drop the Rage, Turn The Page!*

Rage showed itself in this election cycle when people switched parties, switched hopes and aspirations, and became very ugly in how each Party campaigned against the opposing Party. It is time to "turn the page" and move toward healing, compromise where necessary, without unnecessary anger being in the picture.

My intent then for writing this book is to hopefully neutralize the rage around the President being black and Christian, and **"turn the page"** on politically inspired hatred. This hatred that has permeated the news, has caused many Americans to be totally confused on the issues we face today the issues are fixed so as to divide us rather than unite us.

The Midterm Election of 2010 is now over. November 2, 2010 is now history, surrounded by the mystery of the new voting pattern, Anger! Media has had a field day reporting campaign speeches, victories and defeats. The newspapers were quick to pick up the tone of the election: anger, a referendum against President Obama, and his Health Care Plan; he didn't consider the voters and the economy, the papers report, although USA Today on the morning after, made clear that six out of ten Americans wanted health care. It seemed to me, that the other four from the ten counted are in a rage about politics. Could it be the Democratic Party or possibly the Republicans who got us into this and couldn't resolve it?

Page one of USA Today, November 3, 2010 edition headliner on page one said "Voters send angry messages." Page 2A was just as volatile: "Voters take anger to the polls," by Rick Hampson. Why the anger, why the rage? One answer may be in how John Fritze closed his article. He quotes John Pitney, "The 2008 election set the table for 2010" said John Pitney of Claremont-McKenna College in California who once worked at the Republican National Committee. "Expectations for the president were high, and no mortal could fulfill the expectations that a lot of people had…about what (Obama) could do – about healing American politics, reversing global warming, bringing about economic prosperity. So that was the problem."[1]

Rage shows itself when people can't have their way, are disappointed by something or someone, or are mean-spirited and out to get someone they never liked in the first place. They channel or harness all this rage in various ways that can be numerous and negative. Some learn to take their rage, disgust, and work to prove their point without any shred of negative behavior. That is not how 2010 has been. Campaigning has been negative, the Tea Party has been vicious, and there is to me a subtle undertone of distrust of politics no matter who is in control; but in this case, I see signs of racial rage coming through in a pronounced way that magnifies dislike of the President because he is African American.

This book will hopefully address rage as an expression of negative notions and behavior; and hopefully how to turn the page on rage, dismiss it, and use our energies for something positive and productive for America. It is also an opportunity to address religious liberty, as a subject that bordered on hatred of one religion over another and where Muslims can build a Mosque in New York. The book will also deal with race, religion and politics, with religion being the dominant source of bedeviling the democratic process, and how a society can better adjust and overcome when we think God and government; quite different from religion and politics. I do recognize that everyone does not believe in God. Perhaps you will find some light on God's character and concerns before you finish reading this work in its entirety.

---

[1] John Fritze, "Voters Send Angry Messages," in *USA Today November 3, 2010 edition* (McLean, VA) pp. 1A-2A.

The Bible speaks a word about it being permissible to be angry without sinning in the process (Ephesians 4:26). Rage holds grudges and turns into wrathful behavior. Anger can be examined with reason about our dislikes: that helps us drop rage in favor of turning the page and start implementing positive changes for the good.

I will end the book with a few hopeful signals of things we can address in common, work on, and work out in spite of our racial, religious, or political persuasions, with an eye toward eliminating rage and turning the page to become better Americans than we have ever been.

I owe a great deal to God and do not in any way intend to deny my spiritual relation with Him or His people; nor do I seek to separate myself from humanity in general and America in particular, the country of my birth and where my vote and your vote makes a difference.

I hope you will be inspired to turn the page in your own pilgrimage through life with a sense of inspiration.

T. DeWitt Smith, Jr., Author
October 2010,
Atlanta, GA

# Foreword

T. DeWitt Smith, Jr., has written a telling and insightful assessment of "Drop The Rage, Turn The Page". That he has done this with such wisdom only makes his survey the more engaging and compelling.

Perhaps the most arresting feature of this admirable evaluation by Dr. Smith is the clear and unmistakable Christian view which is most evident.

All who read "Drop The Rage, Turn The Page" Will feel an irresistible urge to just this – and to great advantage.

Gardner Taylor, D. D., Pastor Emeritus
The Concord Baptist Church of Christ
Brooklyn, New York

## Chapter One
## Tensions Swirl

When President Obama and New York City Mayor Michael Bloomberg both agreed by saying that it was alright for the Muslim community to build a Mosque, to what others said was dangerously close to Ground Zero where extremists on 9/11/2001 blew up the Twin Towers, and was a blight on moral sensibility and grieving families, President Obama's faith as a Christian became suspect. Tensions began to swirl.

Both Bloomberg (a Jew) and Obama (a Christian) leaned on the facts: the right of people to build a worship center wherever they wanted to, based on freedom of religion in America – a right upheld by the Baptist Joint Committee on Religious Affairs, and many other thoughtful people. The argument is still festering and may never be settled. I only mention it.

My intent for writing is not to argue their points that are now public record. Rather as I said above, I would like to hopefully neutralize the rage around the President being black and Christian, and "turn the page"[2] to see if we can find common ground on our president's prayer life, American life with comments about race and religion, politics and religion, God and government. "Turn the page," is still alive in President Obama's speeches when stomping the country in support of the poor and outcast, the Democratic Party, and what he feels is good for all America. My hope is that we will see what is good for America.

It seems to me that whenever a political figure of the magnitude of our president explains his or her faith journey, there is always a fringe that gets top billing to refute that political figure's belief in God. Faith in God is usually equated with the fringe opposition's definition of redemption that generally runs counter to his or her behavior. It also becomes the tool the media uses to exploit lies or twist the truth with enough sensationalism in favor of great ratings.

Sensationalism still remains on the throne of radio and television talk shows. Thus, any reason will do to disprove the president's faith. President Obama is a man of deep personal piety when it comes to Christ and His Church. Every American president, whether openly or privately has exposed us to an explanation of their faith walk with God Almighty.

---

[1] "Turn the page," is a statement made by then Senator Obama during his campaign speeches when running for President that also were complimented his "Yes we can" statements.

President Obama is not an exception, but a part of a flow of Christianity in the American presidency, whether to the right or left, in their political decisions.

Most recently I listened to an argument of author Dinesh D'Souza, who has written a book entitled *The Roots of Obama's Rage* on the 700 Club on October 7, 2010, which supports his thesis that President Obama can be best understood from reading Obama's book *Dreams From My Father*. He suggests that President Obama is apologizing for America's actions abroad as "the rogue elephant" that has run roughshod and rampant over other nations imposing our will, springs from two reasons. The first reason is that President Obama is intending to bring America into a more neutral position as a player on the world stage, such as Denmark, Sweden, etc., rather than being the number one moral leader of the nations.

And the second reason is his feeling that President Obama may be projecting the dreams for a socialistic America, as desired by his Kenyan father (whom he hardly knew), instead of America as a capitalistic free enterprising nation. Obama's father was a Harvard Grad; so is President Barack Hussein Obama (named after his absentee father). I wonder if education in Harvard pressed his father toward that posture. D'Souza never stated in his interview why, in 2008-2009 the media had been asking the question, "Why so many people hate America?"

This cannot be all there is to President Obama. Much more material will doubtfully come forth in time to support further Republican takeover or a Democratic demagoguery that does not include President Obama in the future. It may also be that the thinking is the Tea Party might move the GOP off the scene in hopes of causing America to politically rebel against this "black" figure of a thinker called our president, as a protest to the GOP not rebelling instead. Such a future move could trigger an end to health care, social security maybe, and big government as conservative extremists call it; all of these reprisals against the first Republican loss of power due to the economic downturn that led to Obama's election.

I suspect as I have in the past when talking with others, some people were willing to hold back disappointment, thus allowing most Americans to celebrate a victory with a first black president. After the Inauguration, negative propaganda from the extreme right signaled they would not cooperate with anything the president does: health care, better incentives for job security. Most of it was due to rage and anger over NOT being a War Lord in Iraq – drawing down troops in the pullout of 2010.

The very fact that our President Obama wants something so close to a decisive defeat of terrorists in Afghanistan, so the troop draw-down can begin in 2011 is a sign that the war-mongers of our present are in total disarray because they can't say "we are still at war, gaining victories that keep democracy free and safe for every American." Continual war only reigns and rages in the hearts of warmongers, who enjoy spending more on war, than ending a war of poverty.

Hopefully, tensions will stop swirling, rage will die down, and Obama will never be assassinated. Besides, that would make him a martyr and would necessitate another "Negro holiday" which the hateful can ill-afford.

The fringe elements however, assassinate his faith, exploit what they say are his socialistic tendencies, and his apology for American aggression. Perhaps an apology is in order and will bring on spiritual revival in our land we love. Repentance always precedes spiritual renewal. America has NOT experienced a major Revival in years. We are in need of a spiritual revival. Most true Christians know that repentance, sorrow, and seeking God bring REVIVAL (see 1 Samuel 7; 2 Chronicles 7:14; Isaiah 55:6-7; Matthew 18:3; Acts 16: 27-31).

It is my hope that we can look at ourselves in light of much of what will shape our political outlook for the future, look at the real person who is our 44th President, look at what we as Americans can do to promote healthy political debate, without unhealthy hatred raging in our speech. It is my prayer that this book can be a transforming instrument of blessing to all of the America public and beyond, but especially a blessing to the people who actively participate in voting to elect all who represent us, no matter what office they hold.

I hope these pages, will ignite spiritual revival, help us get over our political and racial rage, and hopefully come of age on the real issue of race and the God-kind-of relationship that we all need.

Getting over our rage would mean to get beyond the negative Tea Party's covert racist tendencies, and realize that our president's faith is not suspect, but is solid with salvation that is based on the grace of God. That salvation cannot be bought or bargained for, but has to be surrendered to when the Holy Spirit makes it plain we can't get to heaven without Jesus. American fringe elements often support this type of faith but act contrary to it for political expedience in firing up their party's sense of superiority in political life (though not always).

I suggest we stop our rage and turn the page and look at President Obama not only as the leader of the free world, but also as a child of God Almighty, who is unashamedly a Christian whom history will record as a force for good.

14

## Chapter Two
## Who's To Blame

When President Obama was on the Presidential Election Campaign trail, he and John McCain were campaigning during a time that the shift in American politics was about to change forever. Much of it due to finding someone Republicans and Democrats could blame for the economic woes that the country was going through. AIG, Lehman Brothers, Sachs, banks closing, home-building and buying slowing down to a crawl, foreclosures on homes, churches, businesses dying out, was the sign that the end of an American era as we knew it would change.

Everybody needed someone to blame for this. After all, Bernie Madoff had done his worst by misuse of private funds placed in his care by the rich and not-so-rich investors, with a Ponzi scheme that did irreparable damage to the conscience of American investing. Americans were in a debt cycle that was rapidly spiraling downward without any escape hatch to break free from its death grip.

President Bush tried to turn things around by sending checks to all of those in America who deserved it – the American people who worked hard for their money; it was going to be a guarantee to "jump start" the American economy. Checks were sent out through the mail, dollars were received, but people held on to their money because the job market had begun to show signs of a big employment layoff for an indefinite time, and some jobs closing out altogether.

In addition to all of this, the morals of the country spoke to a worsening morale in the people. Life became intolerable as some people began to steal and rob for food – something the experts tell us happens when the economy is in bad shape. How bad? Enough to suggest that we may be plummeting into our Second Depression, much like the one we hear or heard our grandparents talk about. A sense of lawlessness can slip in when people feel all hope is lost.

There was a need to lay the blame at someone's feet. The giants in finance on Wall Street had failed. They stole from their own employees, by lining their own pockets with big bonuses. Wall Street had failed to police its own. Someone was going to have to pay the price for Wall Street greed, for Wall Street sins. "Somebody, anybody," people intoned, had to take responsibility and at least try to do something and do it quick in order to restore public trust! Where's the Congress on all of this, many wondered? During a vote for a Stimulus Package, both Senators Obama and McCain left the Campaign Trail, and went back to Washington to the Senate to give their help.

The Stimulus Package was approved and distributed with good will, but without the sufficient guidelines, and with no effort to police the distribution. It resulted in the financial picture remaining unchanged. People became shaky, the economy worsened, and a presidential election was about to happen that would change the face of American politics when a black man would win the Presidential Election and he and his wife and family would become America's first family – historic indeed.

Obama campaigned on Change. The Democrats were enthusiastic about change. The Republicans admitted that we needed change. Many of them distanced themselves from President Bush during the campaigning, much like we have seen some Democrats do with President Obama during the 2010 Midterm campaigns. Be that as it was, the picture for a healthy America was to be diagnosed and put in the hands of new leadership. America needed Change! Poised, the people made their choice, and then, shortly after Election night and inauguration passed, expected change to happen overnight.

Elections don't change the landscape of economics overnight; people, lawmakers, business, and technology help to change that. Work after the election is where business begins in the halls of Congress, State Houses, City and County Councils across the nation.

But the facts are quite simple. President Obama inherited a failing economy, that was handed over to him by the TAX AND SPEND REPUBLICANS (tag identification on the lapels and feet of the Republican Party instead of the Democratic Party) who were not minding the business of government as they should have. Like Nero, of whom we hear that Rome fell under his administration with the statement, "Nero fiddled while Rome burned;" we may easily say that same statement held true for the TAX AND SPEND REPUBLICANS under the Bush Administration. They dropped the ball, and know it. Consider New Orleans.

New Orleans did not happen as an act of God, as some might think. Benign neglect kept the protection of their citizens, slightly under what was needed to withstand Hurricane category 3 storms. There should be some real rage and indignation about that, with all the people who were displaced, moved out of the Ninth Ward, and removed from New Orleans, in hopes of what many still speculate, is a corporate takeover of the land, without adequate compensation.

Then when President Obama dared to be a take-charge president on all fronts, the sparks of partisan politics began to fly.

People in the Republican Party became calloused and calculating about how to derail the influence of the new president. "Stack the deck against him with negative rhetoric, show the American people that the Democrats aren't worth their salt, and we can get this thing back in our hands. Blame the President for not working with us." Harsh indeed and untrue!

The horrendous Oil Spill that is still being worked out in terms of technology, is not moving fast enough to insure that all of those whose employment came from the waters, where fish and shrimp, and crawfish are famous Louisiana cuisine, is still due to partisan politics on the side of the aisle that most of the rage comes from. The people in Alabama, Mississippi, and Louisiana in the Gulf Region deserve to have the basic necessities of life that they are being denied. And the blame is being played out by the rage of people who point the finger to the American President they wish to discredit the most.

In the meantime, the Democrats seemed to crouch in fear after they had done Americans a service by passing health care. They began to run and hide, not being as cooperative as they needed to be when health care and other legislation passed.

No one was inclined to or seems to have had the inclination within the Congress to see that the ball of bipartisanship was dropped. If the Republicans apologized, if the Democrats apologized; no if Congress apologizes, since they are members from the Democratic and Republican parties, that would be the best thing that could happen. That was not about to happen.

Sarah Palin lost the election bid for the vice-presidency but the right wing extremists entered in to be the catalyst for taking the Democratic movement forward, down funding her popularity in the media. She joined others in further alarming all who were frightened by health care (the Republicans used scare tactics to play on the minds of the elderly and poor people who did not understand how political games can become political gain if played correctly). Extremists helped her do her best to derail the change had America demanded. She has become the spokesperson for a movement called the Tea Party. In the meantime, the Tea Party is fueling the fires of rage, and staging their campaign on a promise to take America to where it needed to be. Back to a limited government, back to individualism, States rights, and all that was dear to the American people. Of course the Tea Party never defined which group of the American people thought America was lost. She would not be a good President; she quit being Governor of Alaska before her term ended: she might do that as President of the United States of America. That would not be good for us.

Tea Party strategists and politics of dissatisfaction have helped to frame the language of blame, while conservative, right wing Radio and Television personalities have helped to fan the flame for the blame. They effectively put the blame on President Obama and those "liberal, tax and spend" Democrats.

With dissatisfaction flaming, the Tea Party began looking for ways to make their argument solid, and bring reproach on the President. The language was vitriolic, "he's un-American:" translated to mean he was not born in America. That was lie number one. Lie number two, his religion is unacceptable: Christianity questioned. Another lie put forward is that Obama doesn't understand the job of president; he was a senator for only four years; he needed more time in the Senate before running. The list is longer, but I will not go further.

Anything that could be done to make his administration look bad has been done. Let their rage begin. The right wing (not all) and the Tea Party have laid most of the blame for the failing economy on the President of the United States of America: Barack Obama. Did media do a great job of reporting everything? No Sir and no Ma'am. Media made it look like the rage over failure of the economy and loss of jobs is justified. Media, in many cases left the window of opportunity open for extremists to take as many potshots at President Obama as they could muster to keep their program ratings alive. Let the rage begin? My thought is that rage must stop, now!

It is time to drop the American rage and hopefully turn the page through positive changes in our hearts and thinking. We can always blame someone else for our troubles. But something good and wholesome happens when we take a look at ourselves, and accept responsibility for some of the blame.

## Chapter Three
## What Evil Has He Done?

When Jesus was brought before Pontius Pilate, implicated by the supreme court of Jewish appeal, indicted by their own Kangaroo Court proceedings in Jerusalem, trying desperately to make their case to the Procurator appointed by Rome, Pilate found himself asking on what evil grounds were they bringing charges. Pilate knew of Jesus' alleged stellar record of free health care, hunger relief, restoration of the dead, and His brilliant teaching career; concern for the least, lost, and left out. Why would the Chief Priest and Scribes and Pharisees want to crucify Jesus? *"And the governor said, Why, what evil hath he done?"[3]*

Pilate's wife helped him extricate himself from the process by telling her husband that Jesus was a just man, and also relating to Pilate her negative dream-state she had experienced that day, because of the proceedings. Pilate followed through with the vindication of his extrication by washing his hands of the matter and telling the Jews (who could not carry out capital punishment without the help and authorization of Rome) to take the matter into their own hands. It is reported from Christian tradition that after Jesus' resurrection and ascension, Pilate (date uncertain) became a believer in the Lord Jesus Christ.

The incident leads me to question the minds of an American system that castigates their leaders, "what evil has President Obama done?" And what do they think he might do that is so damaging to America that the Tea Party continually seems to push the idea, "we have to take America back?" From whom do you propose to take it, and more importantly, where has America gone, so that it needs to be taken back?

It might be helpful to note that America was "taken away" from the Indians. Americans "took slaves" from Africa, brought them to America for servitude, objected to their Emancipation, and in theory promised them forty acres and a mule, but after Emancipation, took back their promise.

So, I again ask, where has America gone? Has it fled to some distant indistinct place that is only visible to those who saw its departure? The last time I looked our borders, though constantly in need of watching and protecting due to the threat of terrorist attacks, are still in tact.

---

[1]See the whole drama played out in Matthew 27(particularly verses 19-23) from which our quote is taken.

President Obama has simply moved in a direction that spells a possible progress in turning the page on traditional Washington partisan politics.

Those who are not in favor of what he is doing are bitter and in a retaliatory mood. He is not the first or the last American president people will disagree with on both sides of the political spectrum. However, when former President George H. W. Bush wanted to go to war in Kuwait, both parties, with the Democratic speaker of the House gave verbal support to the fact that President Bush is the leader of our nation (at that time). Both Democrats and Republican gave support to the President. There is nothing wrong with that, when there is a need for bipartisan support.

However, when it comes to the deficit President Obama inherited, and a Stimulus package that had to be renewed because of Wall Street indulgence and greed, things and people began to divide over the fact that the president had not fixed this as quickly as they thought he should and to their liking.

Big business was suddenly under the gun for ill-gotten gain from the Obama Administration and Congress; this translates into reckless spending habits with excessive bonuses and benefits to the people at the top, while the people in the middle and at the bottom were left behind. Big Business and their practices did not sit well with the American voters. However, President Obama in taking action so swiftly was about to be tried hastily by the media talk show hosts who in turn, passed their quick editions and venomous commentary on to the streets, and finally into the houses of Congress for the purpose of dividing and conquering. The calculated theory was similar to what Joseph's brothers in the Old Testament did to rid themselves of his irksome presence: *let's kill (not literally) the dreamer and see what becomes of his dream.*

President Obama introduced health care reform (special blessings are included for children that have no insurance) that assures we cannot be turned down for pre-existing conditions; children can be retained in their parents' health care program until they are twenty-six years of age (their spouse, under twenty-six is included); what evil has he done? The Congress has until 2014 to tweak the law. If Republicans can have their way, repeal is certain, if they can sway their majority. I feel like using the words of former President William Jefferson Clinton, "mend it; don't end it." When the Health Care Bill was passed, President Obama signed it. When business reform was passed, President Obama signed it into law. Then people started to look for any type of way to bring his presidential reputation into question. I ask again, what evil has he done?

He has presented us with initiatives for building strong families, by he and his wife Michelle modeling it, thereby promoting the sanctity of marriage.

President Obama has pushed for Tax Credits for parents who have adopted children; he has helped the process with tax initiatives for the middle class who have the problem of obtaining tuition for their children who want an education beyond high school; their children can go to college. Dialogue is advancing Technical School and Community Colleges attendance. President Obama has introduced responsible fatherhood initiatives that are helping many American males without fathers become better fathers themselves. He has taken the sting out of abortion, not by ignoring the law but by bringing in alternatives that would stop teen pregnancies, promote adoption of unwanted children, instead of promoting the destruction of the unborn. What evil has he done?

President Obama is not, and I repeat the first, nor will he be the last president people disagree with. As long as there is an America, as long as there is a Democratic and Republican Party, and Independent parties, as long as there is debate in political life, there will be disagreement on issues.

# Chapter Four
## From Vilification to Sanctification

I will never forget the emptiness I felt when the Reverend Franklin Graham, son of respected sage and evangelist Rev. Billy Graham (certainly without the tact of his father), came out on television declaring "Obama is a Muslim." Graham knew better, but seized a media opportunity to confuse public thought and perhaps even (could be a tool of some right-wing financial backers) skew public and political opinion in favor of Conservative Right-Wing extremist politics.

I know that Graham knows better, because he and I both attended a session in April 2008 with then Senator Obama and other Evangelical Faith Leaders in a private meeting where Graham almost without relenting, interrogated then Senator Obama about his journey with Jesus.

I can still hear him inquiring in an almost condescending but badgering tone, to the Senator from Illinois, "Now tell us about *your journey of faith* (italics, mine). You were a Muslim...etc." I asked myself, where are we about to go with this since Senator Obama has already elaborated on his faith in Christ? Graham continued, "Do you believe Jesus is your personal Savior? How did you come to this from your Muslim background, etc.?"

Senator Obama said that "I was never a Muslim (my stepfather was)," and went on to describe that his mother and her parents were nominal Christians – not every Sunday attendees – but were people of moral integrity and good will. "I believe and know Jesus is my Lord and Savior, I believe that the Bible is God's Word...I will leave the rest to you." Graham turned a couple of shades of red; and I thought, "good enough for you for not accepting his answer the first time around."

As we approached the days of debate over whether or not it was right or wrong for Religious Freedom to take its course in the determination of where to build a Mosque in New York, suddenly when President Obama made a comment regarding the process religious liberty takes on, he was under attack from the pundits who shifted the talk from building to what is our President's faith? Graham entered the thicket with his reiteration of doubt about President Obama being a child of God by faith in Jesus Christ.

Below is an excerpt from the ABC news web site I copied and pasted into this document.

**ABC News and World Report on August 20, 2010**

On the heels of a new poll suggesting that nearly one in five Americans incorrectly believes that President Obama is a Muslim, one of the nation's most prominent evangelical leaders has weighed in with a seemingly lukewarm endorsement of the president's Christian faith.

The Rev. Franklin Graham waded into the discussion with his own controversial explanation of why people wrongly believe the president is a Muslim. Graham, who prayed with Obama in a session with his father, Billy Graham, earlier this year, was asked whether he has any doubts about Obama's self-avowed Christian faith.

"I think the president's problem is that he was born a Muslim, his father was a Muslim. The seed of Islam is passed through the father like the seed of Judaism is passed through the mother. He was born a Muslim, his father gave him an Islamic name," Graham told CNN's John King in a televised interview that aired Thursday night. (August 19, 2010 on John King U. S. A.).[4]

One of the difficulties I have with Graham's argument about the Muslim "seed" philosophy is the "spiritual seed" lesson that comes from the Scriptures. 1 John 3: 7-9 clearly states this, *Little children, let no one deceive you. He who practices righteousness is righteous, just as He is righteous. He who sins is of the devil, for the devil has sinned from the beginning. For this purpose the Son of God was manifested, that He might destroy the works of the devil. Whoever has been born of God does not sin, for **His seed remains in him**; and he cannot sin, because he has been born of God.* (NKJ) If President Obama is a confessing Christian, then God's seed is in him, and no matter whom his earthly parents were, Obama is now a child of God.

It would therefore seem to me that a preacher of the Gospel would be the first to embrace the Scriptures as God's Word, using the spiritual argument instead of the physical argument of whose seed any believer is in Christ. God's seed according to this passage is clearly in our president and anyone else who professes Christ as their Savior and Lord; they are indwelt by the Spirit of God, and do not make it their daily practice to sin.

President Obama has had more conversations than I think necessary to convince the American public that he is Christian and that he is for the good of America.

---

4. ABC News and World Report on August 20, 2010. You can view the full report and interview that John King had with Reverend Franklin Graham the night before at the CNN and ABC News web pages.

However, I am disappointed by the fact that some Christians are shaky on the subject of being "saved by grace" (see **Romans** 5:1-2; 8:15, 14-17; **10: 6-17;** Ephesians 2: 8-10 for further amplification). And to prove their shaky inclinations they use whatever message is available and popular enough to vilify and even nullify the President's faith.

The second thought I would want to put to Rev. Graham is "Where is redemption in all of your talk?" I wanted to ask Rev. Graham, "where is the acceptance of a fellow family member of the faith of Jesus Christ?" I do not believe that the Scriptural fact has gone out of existence, that when a person accepts Jesus Christ as his or her personal Savior and allows Jesus to become their Lord, by the Holy Spirit, that person is a new creature in Christ and the old life is passed away (2 Corinthians 5: 17).

I know for a fact that we are saved by grace through faith from Ephesians 2:8-10, God's workmanship in Christ Jesus. I have been assured by the Christian Bible and its many translations that once we accept Jesus as our Savior, we are not only God's children by faith in His Son, but we have eternal life (John 1:12; 3:16; Colossians 1:13-20).

Salvation is not earned – I don't care how many good things you do. We come to salvation through belief that Jesus shed His blood on the cross for us (Romans 6:23; 10:9-17; 1 Peter 2:24) and that His blood is sufficient not only to save us, but to keep us (1 John 1:7; 5:6) after we become believers. Salvation is worked out through our many good deeds we do, but just as we cannot quit being our parents children, neither do we cease being God the Father's children through Jesus Christ, when we come to God on the basis of faith in His Son and not in our own works of righteousness. God accepts us in Christ, the Holy Spirit seals the adoption, and we are forever God's children (Ephesians 1:13-14). No one can cancel our adoption as God's children.

We have the assurance of our rich salvation through Jesus Christ because He protects the investment of God Almighty (John 10:27-30). I love the illustration given by the Reverend Dr. A. Wayne Johnson, pastor of the Morning Star Baptist Church in Portland Oregon from the John 10: 27 passage when he preached the Progressive National Baptist Convention's Retirement Dinner for Dr. Tyrone S. Pitts our General Secretary. He said, and it blessed my soul as I listened. "I believe in the eternal security of the believer." He went on to say, "I can't lose my salvation because I am in Christ, and Satan can't get to me. I am in the hands of Jesus Christ.

Satan has to get past God first…stand before Christ next, peel back the fingers of Christ to get to me, and then walk inside the hands of Christ to get me out. But he can't risk that because once he gets into the hands of Christ, he might be saved."[5] We rose up in the Spirit of the Lord and celebrated our security in Christ. President Obama is a believer in this same Jesus who assures and continues to assure us of our salvation. To say otherwise is to impugn his religious liberty and his faith.

Religious liberty is one of the subjects that is the hallmark of our Constitution's Bill of Rights. Religious Liberty is assured by the First Amendment: "Congress shall make no law respecting an establishment of religion, or prohibiting the free exercise thereof; or abridging the freedom of speech or of the press; or the right of the people to peaceably assemble, and to petition the Government for redress of grievances."

I think that people get off the track about religious liberty when they take it to mean separation of Church and State. It does not read that way. The Church and the State need not intrude on each other: that is the simple less complicated version of Separation of Church and State. And while I am far from any type of expert in Constitutional Law, I can at least read that the First Amendment was addressed to Congress, on behalf of religious freedom, free speech, and a prohibition against Congress favoring a certain religious sect.

I am in disagreement with author Gary DeMar in his defense of America being a Christian nation. I am in agreement however, on a couple of things he says about the First Amendment. "**The prohibition is addressed to Congress** (bold added for emphasis – mine). Individual states and governmental institutions (e.g., public schools, capitol buildings steps, national parks, etc.) are not included in the amendment's prohibition."[6] I am a little uncomfortable with his states rights, but fully understand his defense of the states having the right to promote religion without regard to denomination. He notes elsewhere in his book how states were not interfered with in this area. At the time of the founding of America, the thirteen Colonies were in infancy. DeMar does not deal with the issue of States Rights beyond the subject of religious freedom. So I will leave it to your discretion to read him further.

However he does say on the subject of religious freedom in the Constitution, "There is no mention of a freedom from religion."

---

[5]January 19, 2010 at the PNBC Midwinter Board Meeting in Myrtle Beach, SC.
[6]Gary DeMar, *America's Christian History: The Untold Story.* (Atlanta, GA: American Vision, 1993 and 1995) pp, 147.

The First Amendment offers no support of the position that would outlaw religion just because it offends those of a different religion or those who have no religion at all (agnostics or atheists)."[7] Freedom from religion and freedom of religion are voluntary.

One of my struggles is that when the ACLU promotes a person's right to worship as they choose, it is not too long before they are standing with someone who wants no mention of God or prayer, etc. That sends a confusing signal.

We might well ask how far does freedom of speech go in our church houses of worship, synagogues, and mosques? In the context of the Judeo-Christian Scriptures, one could criticize government without being caustic. The pulpit is an excellent place to share insights about the good and evil of our democratic system. It must not be controlled. The prophets of Israel warned the nation and their kings and counselors to the kings to flee sin. The Christian prophet should do no less.

We talk about freedom, but depending on which party is in charge, religious liberty may be interpreted differently. I am told that the liberal left of the Democratic Party would strip every vestige of God from government if they could. I don't think that is hidden in some of what I read and hear. The Republican extremists on the other hand, would support religious freedom in the pulpit until someone makes a party distinction. Given the fact that both Democrats and Republicans come to the Faith Community for votes is a good thing. However, they should not be willing to support law that hampers religious freedom of any type unless it is hate-filled rhetoric that begins to border on terrorism.

The Church is not the government and never was intended to be. Likewise the Government is not the Church and should not try to be. Both Church and Government should be free to speak, but prohibited from interference into each other's domain. The Faith Community needs to address public policy and warn its parishioners and members of legislation that will go against the grain of Scripture where moral decisions must be dealt with. People are free to do their own thinking and make up their minds about an issue. But where the Church is concerned, the Church should be free to speak prophetically, and "warn the nation" of its sins. Religious liberty is our right, free speech is our right, and it should not be breached or confused by those who wish to abrogate it.

---

[7] Ibid., p. 1148.

There is much talk that America is a Christian nation. I do believe that the prayers of the first settlers on these shores, offered to God to claim America for Christ is still in order, but we are not a Christian nation because we have chosen to respect religious freedom – that invites pluralism. It means people can believe what they choose: God or nothing, Christ or a crystal ball, without the government dictating that they embrace a certain religious practice.[8]

We practice tolerance of the belief of others rather than oppose their religious beliefs. Much like Jesus, the Apostle Paul and Peter, most Christians in America do not force our faith on anyone but pray for the salvation of all, and live life in conformity with God's will, and try to treat people like we want to be treated, hoping the Holy Spirit will bring opportunities to share our faith (1 Peter 3:15).

We have added to our credit elected officials who profess the faith of Jesus Christ the Lord as their faith, not just to get into office, but because they believe in Jesus. Our founders worked out their faith issues under religious freedom legislation, so that our government would not favor a particular religious sect. People are free to worship as they choose. That is a blessing to America. I do know that America needs prayer from people of faith that we all may be saved before Jesus comes.

When we talk about America there are people of many different belief systems that are not Christian. According to William Underwood, President of Mercer University in Macon, GA, "America has never been a Christian nation..."[9] You can read some of his comments online at the Baptist Joint Committee web site. He went on to state a disturbing but true analysis of a serious problem in American life, which in my humble opinion sums up some of our church arguments about faith and flag.

Underwood states that much of what we are labeling as patriotic, might be classified as Christian nationalism. A problem indeed, because it is then not about constitutionality, but about certain personifications of minority extremisms taking over: as in KKK days, or Black rage days in the late sixties of our last century. The defining of America should be about God's goodness to us and that we continue to exist as the leader of the free world, by His grace toward us.

---

[8] See J. Brent Walker, *Religious Liberty and Church-State Separation.* Brentwood, TN: Baptist History and Heritage Society, 2003. This is an excellent book that can inform our thinking on Religious Freedom in America.
[9] William Underwood was the BJC Religious Liberty Award Luncheon and Guest Speaker and Recipient, June 25, 2010 in Charlotte, NC. Heard by this writer, while representing the Progressive National Baptist Convention, Inc.; witnessing Dr. Gardner C. Taylor our President Emeritus also receive the Religious Liberty Award.

Salvation from God is not something we can buy, sell or bargain to obtain. Salvation is the graciousness of God toward us, in sending His only begotten Son to take our sins upon himself along with the punishment called for: dying on the cross – the prevailing form of Roman execution – the curse of the Old Testament lesson spoken about in Romans 5:8; Galatians 3:13-14.

Now this may cause some to chaff, but consider what I say in light of what God can do in American and any other nation. President Obama is God's appointed man for this hour. This was confirmed by a majority vote of the American people in November 2008.The chipping away started shortly after his Inaugural Address. Reading Daniel 4: 34-37 is very instructive and will be readily recognized by Christians and others who adhere to the Judeo-Christian Scriptures where Nebuchadnezzar reports, after his political divinely imposed, hiatus in the wilderness, that God puts in office whomever He pleases. An even larger message coming from Romans 13: 1-8 is that rulers, potentates, presidents, governors, and legislators, need to heed in America, is to realize their appointment by Almighty God is an opportunity for good and not for evil.

If in fact, our presidents for good or ill are placed by God, I have no reason to disbelieve or question this, along with our other political legislators and judiciary (however that is worked out politically), then we should be in prayer for all of them, since we say we are believers. We should pray and hope they will take the opportunity God is giving them to do some good for all Americans.

Our president may very well emerge from of all this as Joseph did, by sitting down with the Tea Party and other extremists, with Democrats and Republicans, as Joseph in the Old Testament did with his brothers who were suspicious that he might take revenge on them. Look at Joseph's answer to them in Genesis 50: 19-20. *"And Joseph said unto them, Fear not: for am I in the place of God? But as for you, ye thought evil against me; but God meant it unto good, to bring to pass, as it is this day, to save much people alive"*(KJV).

## Chapter Five
## When The Rage Is Really Racism

Unfortunately, we cannot escape the subject of race when we talk about the political scene in America. We are still largely polarized by race and ethnicity. Even if the gap is closing, we still have a long way to go to completely close it. There are some people who want to escape race in politics; they will not escape. Race has been a historical portion of American politics from the days of the American Revolution forward. I was always taught to speak of things as they are. So I will say it. Race is still a problem in America.

There were even Liberals who perpetuated race dominance by believing in the slave trade and sustaining Negroes remaining chattel. We do not always want to face the truth, but this is true. "What was left out of the historical accounting was the role of American liberalism as a collaborator, by acquiescence or default, with American racism."[10] Race has not died out and probably won't for a long time.

One new group on the scene has decided to be Frederick Douglass Republicans who do not consider themselves conservatives, as it is defined by many in the Republican Party. According to Retired Army officer Fred Smith, a Frederick Douglass Republican "breaks through the racial barriers, and believes in limited government and respects Constitutional life."[11]

They say it is a way to discuss social issues without bringing in *Race Issues* – italics, mine. Frederick Douglass was a Black man, a Republican, and was extended the opportunity to run for Vice President during his lifetime with the Republican Party, which he turned down of course.

This new Alabama-instituted group is to its credit inclusive of non-blacks. However, I do not see how they can really escape the subject of race, when it comes to politics in American life, because we are still a severely racially divided nation.

A case in point as an illustration of my thoughts is how former President Carter understood the political unrest in our country shortly after Obama took office. All the media, Right-winged extremists included, picked up on former President Jimmy Carter's statement that what was happening to President Obama was

---

[10] Samuel DuBois Cook (Editor). Howard Zinn, "American Liberalism: Source of Negro Radicalism" in *Benjamin E. May, His life, contributions, and legacy* (Tennessee: Providence House Publishers, 2009.
[11] Introduced on a news edition of the 700 Club, October 2010.

actually about "race." Conservatives recoiled at that idea that it was about race, but President Carter had his hand on the pulse of negative politics and diagnosed it accurately.

I quote here President Carter's words from his interview with Brian Williams on September 15, 2009.

> "I think an overwhelming portion of the intensely demonstrated animosity toward President Barack Obama is based on the fact that he is a black man," Carter said. "I live in the South, and I've seen the South come a long way, and I've seen the rest of the country that share the South's attitude toward minority groups at that time, particularly African Americans." President Carter continued, "And that racism inclination still exists. And I think it's bubbled up to the surface because of the belief among many white people, not just in the South but around the country, that African-Americans are not qualified to lead this great country. It's an abominable circumstance, and it grieves me and concerns me very deeply."[12]

People have a difficult time with this thing called *Race*. Some people who cannot stand knowing that the President of the United States of America is black, mixed of Kenyan and Kansas parentage, have put forth the argument, I reiterate, "we need to take back America."

America is supposed to be the bastion of democracy. It is the place where if any good can happen, it will happen in our land. It was always an accepted fact that the presidency belonged to the white race and no other race. But we preached opportunity, even to black people, and someone grabbed it.

It has always been an accepted theory that the presidency of the United States of America belonged to "white men" but it looks like that theory might be disproved in the near future after President Obama. It has been accepted theory that the presidency belonged to whites only, not to non-whites.

The idea that follows is also a theory some people are careful not to utter aloud, let alone recognize.

If American remains true to its promise that America, the "Land of Opportunity" is for All Americans then anything is possible, especially, when climbing the ladder to success is concerned. Since a black man has become our 44th President, there is

---

[12] From NBC's Mark Murray First Read from NBC News. Article posted entitled, **"Carter: Race plays role in Obama dislike."** In an interview with NBC's Brian Williams, former Democratic **President Jimmy Carter** attributed much of the conservative opposition that **President Obama** is receiving to the issue of race. September 15, 2009. Copied from web page.

a chance, an opportunity for a Hispanic American, Asian American, Jewish American, etc., to become our president.

Most of us can remember that no Catholic was ever supposed to be president, but John F. Kennedy overcame it and became the President. The possibility for other ethnic minorities to become the President of the United States of America is now an open fact that cannot be closed in our future conversations on race.

Being black in America is a miracle of survival. President Obama is one of the few African Americans, who is a "true African American" without a "Bill of Sale" in his background. When he viewed the African West Coast where the slave ships brought unwilling Africans to America, traded into slavery – by war and European greed – by capturing warring tribes that were sold off by the victorious chiefs who held their prisoners in bondage for trinkets and dollars from the white slave traders, I am certain it touched his heart.

When President Obama saw where the doors of African Castles on the slave shores were closed forever to the West African coasts natives, taking African families, dividing them and separating them; shoving them out of the doors of the slave castles into ships launching the now infamous Middle Passage, I am sure, by his statements in the News, he was touched with a new sense of appreciation for his own heritage.

He however, has to help his children understand their maternal heritage. Through no fault of her own, our First Lady has a "Bill of Sale" in her background. For that fact so do I, and millions of Americans whose greater grandparents were transplanted from African shores into American servitude as slaves – someone else's property.

The catch in all of this for people who use race to keep others down with their theories of dominancy and supremacy, is that President Obama was elected by a wide range of people from all the races that make up America. Some supremacists can't stand this and will pay anyone to help fuel their argument that Obama, a black man in our Nation's "White House" is not godly, and that America is losing track with her godly heritage. They are wrong in their assumptions.

What they spew out is mean-spirited rhetoric, powered by dollar signs that help feed their frenzied vocabulary into the American public for Radio and Television Talk Show ratings based on sensationalism and sentimentality, rather than truth.

They will do anything to fire up a controversy. Thank God, it is not the first time a president has received the blunt end of American hatred, and Obama won't be the last. Almost every president after each election bears, his own burden of indignation from people who disagree with his actions in leading the nation; but in the case of President Obama, the rhetoric and parades have been racist inspired.

The 2010 Midterm nation-wide elections **were not about** taking American back, they **were about turning America back** to her pre-1950's position on race.
The pre-1950s attitude was, "let's not deal with the Negro problem; ignore it (them) and it (they) will go away." There is sufficient evidence to commend that I am telling the truth.

We watched only recently, as Shirley Sherrod was portrayed in the media as biased and hateful toward white people. A man named Andrew Breitbart took a video of Sherrod speaking, and fixed it to look as though Sherrod was sharing that she hated white people. It was his negative perpetration of this portrayal that caught the eye of the nation. **It was a racist tactic and an attempt to embarrass President Obama and the Obama Administration.**

The video was far from the truth. It was a twisting of the truth into a lie that swept the nation's televisions and web sites. Sherrod was a member of the Obama Administration. There was a full-scale push from the right wing to get her out as quickly as possible. Again, I repeat, hoping someone will pay attention. **It was a racist tactic and an attempt to embarrass President Obama and the Obama Administration.**

In the wake of her stepping down, someone got a hold of the real video which really told the truth of how God showed her all rage against the past with its history steeped in racism against Negroes and her family caused her to see it as her mission to help a white farmer that was in need of her work: saving his farm. He (the white farmer-Roger Spooner) was greatly benefited by her help.

When confronted with his lie, Breitbart did the predictable thing: refused to apologize for his sin and continued his racist exploitation of the NAACP, and other groups he wants on the radar that paint black faces and minority sympathizers as the evil people "he" wants them to be. This is rage channeled through racism.
Racism raised its head in the senatorial campaigning of Nevada. We heard in a news report, Senator Harry Reid's Republican opponent Sharron Angle, being reported as saying she does not like Presidential Proclamations. The news reporter mentioned one in particular: The Emancipation Proclamation, signed by Abraham

Lincoln. That meant if she became the Senator from Nevada, I might be put back in slavery. President Obama would not be turned out of the White House and returned to slavery because nothing in his parentage has American slavery attached to it.

There is more to this unfortunate form of negative campaigning. Some of it shows up when one may not necessarily intend for it to show up.
Angle also said on October 19, 2010 in a statement to young Latino students captured by someone with a cell phone and video (it's called a "Gotcha" moment) that she could not necessarily say all of the students looked "Latino…some of you might be Asian."[13] It was the feeling of the media that she lost the Latino vote with that statement.

Senator Reid came back on camera at a rally where he spoke declaring, "You all look like Nevadans to me."[14] The crowd applauded with enthusiasm.

Senator Reid was wise to shift the sentiment to all people, and in doing so pointed to the obvious in his opponent, race really was an issue with her or else she would not have made such a comment about it, on or off the camera. He won the November 2, 2010 Election and was returned to Washington to lead the Senate.

When we can face our racial biases with honesty as President Obama did when he was running for office and did that brilliant speech in Philadelphia, many of us will find the healing necessary within ourselves to contribute to the conversation in a way that does not reflect hatred for skin color. Perhaps we are making some progress, but not enough. We are still too fearful of minority races in America.

Author and Harvard professor Clifton Taulbert says that "Although our country has made great strides…our communities still face hardships…The rhetoric of intolerance flashes like lightning across our land, dimming our best dreams."[15] He makes an appeal for what he calls nurturing attitudes in the chapter called Nurturing Attitude.

In Taulbert's chapter entitled Brotherhood, he knows that people are not as quick to be brotherly (or sisterly for that fact) in our community building efforts. He encourages us to take the time to overcome our bondage to fear. Taulbert calls for that forthright determination to make a change. Taulbert decries the fact that some

---

[13] ABC News and CNN reported the story.
[14] Ibid. All a part of the same report on Election Campaigning.
[15] Clifton Taulbert, *Eight Habits of the Heart* (New York: Penguin Books, 1997), p. 21.

are "Afraid to face a world where time, space, and respect must be shared, they hold their "town hall" meetings in fields, hiding their faces under sheets, their agenda unchanged since my boyhood days."[16]

There comes a point in our American experience that we must see that we have an opportunity to drop the rage about racism with its ugly bent toward white or black, or Latino, or Asian supremacy, and turn the page, leaving behind an ugly past and writing a new chapter on integrity. We must begin to progress to the point that we can honestly and earnestly celebrate our racial and ethnic differences and move forward.

I am reminded of what one white gentleman who will remain nameless in Georgia, said to me regarding Obama and Carter. "I like Senator Obama, but I am afraid they will do him just like they did President Jimmy Carter." I asked, "What's that?" He said, "Elect him and then sit on him." I believe that while some in our Congress have tried to sit on President Obama because they cannot stand knowing we have a black president, it is time they stop sitting and start serving the American people who elected them.

It is time to drop the rage and turn the page and celebrate the fact that we have an American president who is concerned about all of the American people, not just the privileged few. It is time we ask God Almighty to forgive us our racism, and start working across the aisles regardless of their Party affiliations, and do what is best for America.

---

[16] Ibid., p. 51.

## Chapter Six
## The Prophet Has A Right To Speak

### God, Black Churches, and the Media

Black worship is different but it has never been exclusionary. We have opened our churches to people of all races even when it was not acceptable for us to be included in their church settings. As one of my relatives put it, when we could not get into white churches we had to have our own churches to worship in. And I add, that many times others came to our churches under pretense of hearing our good singing; but many left hearing a word from the LORD that changed their lives, even if they were present to spy out our liberty. What they heard was prophetic, preaching in the African American tradition.[17]

President and Mrs. Obama, their children, and family members and staff, should be able to worship where they please. They should be able to worship in a black church where strong prophetic preaching and fervent worship are the hallmarks of the African American spiritual journey, or in a white church, where they are welcomed and comfortable, or any church setting of their choice. Since all of our past Presidents of America were white, no one has come forth to condemn them for where they worship. They have had "freedom of worship." How about President Obama? Should not he and his family have this freedom of worship, without media frenzy about him and his family's faith tradition? His spiritual experience is with black worship and prophetic preaching traditions that go back to the days of slavery. It is the type of preaching that is holistic, unbiased, and practical for facing the everyday experiences of our contemporary journey.

Prophetic preaching in the black church always seeks to keep hope alive in the millions who still come to the church building listening for "a Word from the LORD," through their pastors. Insightful prophetic preaching from the African American church (and from any other ethnic church faith tradition) is grounded in the Biblical tradition of advocating for God, sharing His mind and His will, through the voice of the preacher to those in the pews, who will listen and those who are not in the pews and listen to what the Lord is saying to the nation and to the world. It has been reported in our churches that this kind of insightful preaching deals with the times and helps our people live.

---

[17] Note to the reader. This is no way implies that African American churches and their pastors are locked into on type of message. There are pastoral messages, evangelistic messages, mission-driven messages; the black pulpit while one of variety in its preaching, has often been identified in America as having a strong sense of the prophetic tradition so necessary to conditions that shape or destroy the black community.

We have experienced and witnessed, in the span of a few days, what many of us have dubbed as Media Mania Days (2010), and how, so it appears to me, that negative type of reporting in the media sought to destroy then Senator Barack Obama's opportunity from becoming President of the United States of America. We saw the news media work overtime, on the air and on "the Net," to bring back from death, revived video sound bytes from a prophetic sermon Dr. Jeremiah Wright preached in 2001, following the terrorists' attacks on the Twin Towers in New York, and attempted destruction in Washington on September 11, 2001. That was a time Americans saw the need to turn to God and ask Him to heal America.

We will never forget, Congress on the steps of the Capitol building in Washington, D. C. singing "God Bless America." This song has become the watchwords of our seventh inning stretch at baseball games – America's favorite pastime. Now the media, CNN and Fox News in particular, carried Dr. Jeremiah Wright's sound bites so much, it became Continuous Negative News.

Much was being made of this sermon because "it seemed to" invite God Almighty's condemnation on America, so some commentators say.

Then the media brought on the Christmas message of December, in which the media says, retiring Pastor Jeremiah Wright spoke in a disparaging manner about politics by comparing **then Senator, now Secretary of State** Hillary Clinton's experience with Senator Barack Obama's experience as a black man in a white dominated America. Media fell just short of saying Wright endorsed Senator Obama. In Dr. Wright's message, from the looks of it, and many of us have not heard the full sermon or its proposed context.

We do not know what brought on his fiery and insightful illustration suggesting that Senator Clinton has never been a black person denied certain basic recognition by a system that can be exclusionary. Dr. Wright, in these few moments, said nothing incendiary or racist about Senator Clinton. He simply realized, as a sermon illustration, that Senator Obama did not fit the model of popular opinion polls for presidency.

His reason was that the system is controlled by "rich white people," and Senator Obama is a black man. That small portion we heard was and is a fact. I fear there are those who wanted the media to portray Obama as totally unelectable at that time and now, if Senator Mitch McConnell's statement holds up to make President Obama a one-term president, shame. Obama was elected 44th President of the United States of America.

# God Chooses and Positions Prophets

To be sure, there are and will be prophets who bring shame on the bride of Christ. Dr. Jeremiah Wright does not fit that tradition. Those who bring shame on Christ and the Church of God are not part of this discussion; they will receive their rewards for being deceptive. I speak here in this document, of prophets who are right, because they are God's prophets.

God Almighty, by His Holy Spirit, calls and chooses prophets. They are anointed and positioned by God to preach "good news" to people in every nation. Luke 4:18 gives the prophet marching orders – that verse is Jesus' mission statement about His own prophetic ministry. True prophets of God are right because they yield to the irresistible call of God to share His message with sinners and saints.

God's prophets are right because they challenge us from God's perspective, to live lives that reflect God's demand and ideal for justice, mercy, and equity in the land. True prophets of God encourage us to not only love God and love our neighbors as we love ourselves, but they also challenge us to live up to our faith and not beneath our privileges.

Prophets are often unpopular and without honor *"in their own country,"* according to our Lord Jesus Christ, the Ultimate Prophet (see John 4:44). The media has had a field day attacking the prophet whose name is Wright. Was he right? Let me answer like this. A true prophet of God always has the right to speak "thus saith the LORD." True prophets of God may be painful and sometimes harsh in their assessment of current situations, but they also provide the soothing words that bring healing when we have accomplished God's design for a communal life that is fair and just.

True God-sent prophets are not preaching for the personal applause of people and popular opinion polls. They preach to bring God's correction and God's blessing to culture, and without question, their intent in preaching is always centered on bringing glory to God Almighty. Yet, in American pulpits, when the public media hears the prophet and is allowed to determine what the prophet is, or as in Wright's case, determines what he was trying to say, the prophet's voice is often distorted, or his/her words twisted so that there is if possible, a silencing of the prophet's voice.

In some cases, when prophets speak, they are summarily considered, off the correct political path with their comments; and yet, true prophets are powerful voices in

American church pulpits. What seems apparent to me is that **many in the news media (not all)** do not understand the black church worship experience.
They also do not understand the spiritual power of prophetic preaching when it comes from the black pulpit. Black preaching is both convicting and comforting.

I am sure there are marked differences in black and white prophetic delivery styles, because of the focus of the message and the people that prophets preach to. We have this one thing in common, when some prophets condemn sin in America, they are sometimes castigated on the news for their views; yet, they are powerful voices in American church pulpits. In the black church, true prophets are held in high esteem because they liberate God's people to see God's truth.

Some non-black prophets do not prophesy along the same lines of liberation and social justice, and doing social action as our spiritual responsibility, in the same manner as black prophet–pastors have been known to do (Amos 5:24). Yet those who are not black are prophets of God to their own people. My comments about their content are limited to a few thoughts that might be helpful in assessment of their message and style.

At times, their messages are seemingly *accommodating* (my thoughts), baptizing corporate culture, in an effort to remain comfortable. There are times their preachments will deal with feeding the hungry or clothing the naked, but perhaps they do not deal consistently with controversial social issues such as race, because they have no frame of reference, perhaps, to deal with it in an objective manner (this is not necessarily a judgment, but an observation). I do not however, agree with everything every prophet says, and do not hesitate to point out that some in the dominant race speaking prophetically for God, don't always go all the way in preaching against our corporate sins as a nation. They should not stop with preaching on one sin, they should go all the way.

For example, when John Hagee talked about the sin in New Orleans, in the aftermath of the terrible New Orleans fight to survive the devastation of the Hurricane, in my thinking, he should have gone further, to condemn sin in America, because he was referring to the deterioration of public and private morality.

I feel, he should have gone further with evangelical and prophetic fervor to deal with sin all over America in our rural and urban habitations.

Being evangelical does not stop you from being prophetic: it saves people from sin and turns the nation to God. So I say, don't stop at New Orleans, go further; deal with corrupt political systems that hold people down.

Don't stop, go further and deal with corporate greed that denies its workers basic health care, secure employment and advancement possibilities.

Go all the way and deal with those who withhold from their workers a decent wage with a comfortable retirement; don't just condemn the War on Iraq (Some American fighting forces were moved out of Iraq this past Summer 2010), but pray for the safety and security of our Armed Forces who are left behind as peacekeeping forces because they have to assist the Iraqi Government. Local Christians are in harm's way because of Muslim extremists threats on the lives of local Christians in their cities. Killing must stop in Iraq and in Afghanistan. There needs to be some preaching about this as well.

Go all the way. Be prophetic all the way: condemn sin, and then offer God's solution for repentance and healing. This is not just for black preachers only; it is for all preachers of every ethnic origin who must be prophetic in the Christian faith.

## Our Need For Spiritual Revival

God's message, so amply pulled on when America wants to pray is 2 Chronicles 7:14. It speaks to the people of God in the days of the dedication of the Solomon's temple, and to us about the need to seek God when life has fallen apart due to the sins of the nation. The passage evokes (stirs up) prophetic preaching and demands a prayerful public response.

Americans have used it for national days of prayer through the years but have never fully embraced all that it calls for, or to obey all it refers to: we want the healing, but we will not do what is required to receive the healing. The passage says what God says, but we have not done all that He has called for in that passage.

As a result, our land stands in need of a spiritual, moral, and ethical revival that will bring the desired healing so necessary to a sinful and wayward people. America has not really had a revival since the days of the Civil Rights movement when spiritual revival brought about some positive moral, social, and political changes. America again needs reviving. Our moral authority is eroding because we do not like to admit our wrongs. Prophets of God help usher in true revival.

Prophetic preaching, undergirded by strong prayer power from the saints in the seats, brings about the much needed spiritual renewal and change that America is overdue to receive, when she turns and obeys God.

The truth is, America has not lived up to her belief that she is one nation under God. We say we are one nation under God from our lips, but it does not really come from our hearts, where decisions are made to commit to God Almighty.
We do not have a strong and abiding use for God in our lives except now and then (i.e., in times of national disasters). In those moments we suddenly and conveniently feel we can fit Him into our lives, we do it knowing we are sinful and pernicious.

We then quickly repent, hoping He will make sense out of our failures, because we have finally recognized we need Him. America needs God. America needs revival. Prophetic preaching underscores that need.

One of the ways you can tell that America needs revival of a true spiritual nature is that killing has not stopped on our streets. Many among us are suffering loss of jobs and loss of homes due to corporate greed and less-than-honest mortgage dealings. For many, paying the mortgage has become a nightmare, due to lack of income. It seems that more drugs and violence are pumped into our veins and brains than dollars into our economy. We are living as a constant battlefield of contradictions. Our children are killed almost faster than they can be born, grow up, and achieve their God ordained purpose for them in the world.

### Strong Prophetic Preaching in the African American Church
A Past and Present Perspective

Strong prophetic preaching deals candidly with these issues, gets under your skin and causes you to think, meditate, repent to God and anyone else you have wronged, and then turn from any form of wickedness that goes against *"Do justly, love mercy, and walk humbly with thy God"* (Micah 6:8).

Strong prophetic preaching is a vital part of the African American church and the lives of our people. Strong prophetic preaching has always been that way since we were the invisible church whose preachers were carefully watched and screened by the plantation masters, and now that we are organized churches gathered under our respective denominational and nondenominational umbrellas.

Our preaching has affected those we lead who sit in the pews, to believe that we as a people, can rise to those heights, God has intended for us all throughout our past, and is now available in our present. There are White Independent Churches engaged in prophetic preaching, as well. My focus here is on the African American Pulpit. African American prophetic preaching has really believed and promulgated the strong theological position that our God is able to deliver us, not only from something distasteful and dreaded as a fiery furnace, but He is also able to deliver us to places and positions we only dreamed about, and are now attainable. African American pulpits abound with prophetic preaching that inspires our parishioners to strive for excellence because God is the Author of excellence, and our only authentic Model for excellence.

Prophetic preaching from black church pulpits has inspired countless families to send their children to school; taught people to reach for ownership as opposed to being constant consumers; prophetic preaching from black pulpits has encouraged our listeners to learn the political system, engage it and run for public office through it, without taking on any hint of its rotten and corrupt nature.

Prophetic preaching has taught us to take on systemic racism, learn its roots and its inherent sicknesses, to challenge it, without being sucked in by it. Indeed, because of prophetic preaching, from African American pulpits, we are continually celebrating our ability to "overcome today and forever." As in the Scriptures, so in the contemporary context of every generation, prophetic preaching encompasses both prediction and proclamation. In prophetic preaching, the future is often tied to "the now," and our progress is determined by how we respond to "thus saith the LORD."

Prophetic preaching in the African American tradition relies heavily on the Scriptures for sure theological footing and sound exhortations. Prophetic preaching is defined by sound exegesis, with a real understanding of the audience, the Scripture is speaking to, in its historical context, and then it goes on to determine what God wants said to the audience that is listening to an ancient message in our contemporary setting. Such preaching is always filled with illustrations that make the message live.

There is never an attempt in the prophetic preaching of the African American pulpit to make a Scripture text say something it does not say. There is always an effort on the part of the preacher/prophet to lift up the message that is present, and preach that which is to be conveyed for today.

Black preaching in and of itself, tends to be fiery, factual, inspiring, and filled with prophetic wisdom for the times, with instructions about living out our faith in relationship to current issues. I'm sure that if everyone listened to the messages preached by Dr. Jeremiah Wright in their entirety, there would be a better appreciation for what was said.

Senator Obama, now President Obama had the right to feel he must disagree and condemn the two messages. The two messages did not fit into his campaign of a new America, where the things Dr. Wright talked about should now be nonexistent. The media or anyone else beyond the media should have never required Senator Obama to defend his relationship with his pastor and friend.

For the simple reason that because Senator Obama did not go along with what everyone said who wanted to give him public endorsement, he has been free to move forward, and do as he intended, be President of everyone: those he agrees with and those he disagrees with.

It is a shame that the media, and many others were insistent on then Senator Obama disassociating himself with his pastor of over twenty years. Some in the media are now and never will be content for things to be left just they are, with what Senator Obama has said regarding Dr. Wright and him.

Many pundits still feel that the media must dig deeper into what else Dr. Jeremiah Wright may have said, or did not say, to clear up his meaning. *After Senator Obama's brilliant defense of his family, faith, and politics, before a watching nation, things moved forward with his campaign. The prophet should be left to preach and turn people to God.

Pastor Jeremiah Wright resigned from the Campaign but not from life. He continues to preach in pulpits across this country and the world, lectures on College and Seminary campuses, wherever opportunity takes him. Dr. Jeremiah Wright is considered one of the great voices of the African American pulpit.

## Stand For Right And Remain Free

Now the question might be asked, should black pastors and preachers have pulled away from Barack Obama to show we have the power to influence the votes in our pews, and punish him for denouncing his pastor?

That is exactly what the devil, some democrats for Hillary Clinton, and some in the Republican Party for Senator John McCain wanted us to do. With Barack Obama out of the picture, John McCain would be "a shoe in." It did not happen in totality.

I happen to know that many stood with Dr. Wright without forsaking Senator Obama. We cannot abandon Dr. Wright or any other true prophet of God, black or white, Native American, Hispanic, or Asian to the press, to be continually lynched by sermon illustrations that do not reflect the total message. We must share God's displeasure from our pulpits without the lynching of prophetic preaching and His Church.

What the Psalmist reflected on Israel's journey in the passage below, still rings true for the Church, today *"...Do not touch My anointed ones, and do My prophets no harm"* (Psalm 105:15 – NKJV). We stood with Wright for what is right. To abandon him, would have been to abandon who and what God has called us to be: prophets who preach His word.

To abandon prophetic preaching would be to kill the liberating freedom the message of the African American pulpit in particular, and the Church in general, has brought to so many oppressed people: people who do not seek, or will ever be able to run for public office. Prophetic preaching also maintains the right to raise people from the pews to be in politics.

And even if the sound bytes were Wright's whole message, he and his former church, and any other pastor and church have the right to be the Church in the context of their community. That's religious freedom, and freedom of speech.

Prophetic pastors are to be free to preach to their people, and for their people to listen to them without the censorship and intrusion of negative politics and the press. Trinity United Church of Christ is a church congregation meeting the needs of its neighborhood and members, much, if not all of this due to the fiery, insightful, and instructive preaching and leadership of Dr. Jeremiah Wright.

We should do what our forefathers did; they were preachers who preached hell out of the lives of their membership and heaven into the lives of our disenfranchised greater grandparents who listened for a way out of slavery, Jim Crow, and segregation of the worst type, whose descendants waited to see a man become president, who happens to be African American: those preachers stuck together and lifted each other.

True prophets of God should never be left abandoned or to feel they are alone, to say as Elijah complained to the LORD, *"I, even I only, am left; and they seek my life, to take it away"* (1 Kings 19:10, 14). We must encourage them as the LORD God told Elijah in his moment of loneliness and despair. God told him, *"Yet I have left Me seven thousand in Israel, all the knees which have not bowed unto Baal, and every mouth which hath not kissed him"* (1 Kings 19:18).[18]

We stood with Jeremiah Wright, and said, "Preach the Word, prophet. Interpret the times for us." We can stand with Dr. Jeremiah Wright and any other prophet of God without forsaking Presidential candidates. There is no sin in that.

There is also no sin in requesting all black and minority people who are blessed to rise and occupy high government office, to never forget that so many pastors like Dr. Jeremiah Wright fought for, marched for, and prayed for them to obtain high office. We need to remind them that Dr. Martin Luther King, Jr. whose assassination on April 4, 1968 we observe annually, was a prophet, and prophesied with such power that his preaching struck a cord of repentance in government and changed the voting and civil rights landscape of American privilege, even though we believe, he was later killed for his views on the War in Vietnam.

We should tell our black and minority elected officials to respect our prophets and respect our churches. We should be unafraid to tell them that, "Such prophets and their people which you have wooed for votes, have opened the doors of opportunity for you to walk through, to your rise to power and the influence you now hold."

It was this type of prophetic insight into the Scriptures that showed the downtrodden multitudes, that prophetic preachers have been privileged to pastor, that there is a hope that lies ahead through perseverance, prayers, and power of our faith, and the power of our going to the ballot box.

### What Type of Prophets Should We Be?

What type of prophets should Christian prophets be who preach in predominantly African American churches? African American history is filled with many great examples to choose from. All have their particular tie to history.

---

[18] Personal pronouns are capitalized by as a reverence for God.

We remember Gabriel Prosser, Nat Turner, and Denmark Vesey who lost their lives for their independent prophetic tradition.[19] We can move in the prophetic-pastoral traditions of the Reverend George Liele, Bishop Richard Allen, Rev. Andrew Bryan,[20] Rev. Adam Clayton Powell, Harriet Tubman, Sojourner Truth, Bishop Charles H. Mason, Bishop Gilbert E. Patterson, Doctors William Augustus Jones, Jr., Nelson H. Smith, Jr., Dr. Vernon Johns, Rev. Joseph Boone, Dr. Ralph David Abernathy.

Or we can adapt the academic posture of Doctors Henry (still living) and the late Ella Mitchell; Dr. Howard Thurman, and Dr. Charles Boddie. They have all passed into eternity with others not mentioned here.

We can move in the powerful, profound and practical prophetic tradition of Doctors Gardner Calvin Taylor, Otis Moss, Jr., Pastor E. D. Smith, Sr., Rev. E. Dewey Smith, Jr.; Bishop Vashti McKenzie, Rev. Jesse Jackson, Dr. Joseph E. Lowery, Rev. Otis Moss, III, Doctor Susan Johnson Cook, Bishop Charles Blake, Dr. Charles G. Adams, Bishop John Bryant, Dr. Barbara Williams-Skinner, Rev. Floyd Flakes, Dr. A. Lincoln James, Jr., Dr. Leonard Smith, Rev. Al Sharpton, and countless other contemporaries whose names are too numerous for this document.[21]

I grew up in Chicago, IL, where the spiritual prophetic tradition was always wedded to social and political activism. I am told, that the late Dr. L. K. Williams and the Olivet Baptist Church housed and fed those who fled the South during the Great Migration north, and that L. K. Williams would personally go to the train station to pick up those persons arriving from the southern states, and make them feel a sense of belonging to their new surroundings. I will never forget the Rev. C. J. Rodgers of the Greater Mt. Eagle Baptist Church, he was a literally a "wasp in the collar" of the government in criticizing the plight of the Little Rock Nine, and Governor Faubus. The Rev. Louis Boddie at the Greater Harvest Baptist Church was feeding the hungry and clothing the naked when things were tough for many, when that type of social ministry was not widespread.

Boddie would say, "You can't tell anybody about Jesus and their stomachs are empty." People would bring canned goods to Greater Harvest to feed the hungry.

---

[19] See Eugene Genovese, *Roll, Jordan, Roll: The World the Slaves Made* (New York, Vintage Books, pp. 593-597). He gives an assessment of the preaching traditions of Prosser, Turner, and Vesey

[20] Read the story of Reverend Andrew Bryan in the book *First Bryan 1788-2001written and copyrighted by Charles J. Elmore in; published by the First Bryan Baptist Church in Savannah, GA, 2002.*

[21] See Marvin A. McMickel, *An Encyclopedia of African American Christian Heritage (Valley Forge: Judson Press, 2002.)* I also commend this for your reading and research. He offers a valuable contribution to the Church.

Social and political activism was often pitted against political gradualism in Chicago, when it came to giving voice to the Civil Rights Movement. I remember clearly that the Rev. Doctors W. N. Daniel (Antioch Baptist Church), Clay Evans (Fellowship Baptist Church), A. Patterson Jackson (Liberty Baptist Church), and John L. Thurston (New Covenant Baptist Church) and others were at the forefront of the Civil Rights Movement, along with other pastors in the city, with their physical presence and pastoral support, and the support of their congregations, allowing Dr. Martin Luther King, Jr. and Dr. Ralph David Abernathy a clear voice to come in, to challenge and bring down the prevailing view that housing was to stay segregated. Their successors have carried on that same activism: Reverends Gerald Dew (Antioch), D. L. Jackson (Liberty), Charles Jenkins (Fellowship), and Dr. Stephen J. Thurston (New Covenant) who currently serves as the president of the National Baptist Convention of America, International.

Dr. W. N. Daniel and Dr. John L. Thurston dared to desegregate a Cemetery that had been the sacred burial grounds of "White Only," when some of their parishioners who lived on the Southside of Chicago near the cemetery could not bury their dead, and would have to go to suburban Burr Oak and Lincoln Cemeteries where my grandparents are buried. They opened the way for all of that to change.

From the Scriptures we have prophets of the likes of Moses, Samuel, Gad who is called the Seer; we can focus on the style of Elijah and Elisha; Isaiah, Jeremiah, Ezekiel, Daniel, and all of the written traditions of the twelve Hebrew prophets, often referred to as Minor Prophets. Their prophetic works in print are by no means minor in content.

In the New Testament, we have unnamed prophets from Jerusalem in whose company Agabus was prominent; Paul and Barnabas and those who were prophets and teachers; we most assuredly not forget Peter and John; John was exiled due to the fact that his prophetic preachments brought imprisonment on Patmos Isle.

Dr. J. Alfred Smith, Sr. is quoted as saying; *perhaps the style of Nathan who preached to David is more suitable than the style of John the Baptist* who got his head cut off.[22] The one thing that I remember about Nathan's prophetic style most is that he had the ear of the king. The black church prophet has often had the ear of our leaders if for no other reason, politicians needed them to turn out the vote.

---

[22] Dr. J. Alfred Smith, Sr. is the Pastor of the Allen Temple Baptist Church in Oakland, CA, whose church is a contemporary model of spiritual, prophetic and social activism.

The Black church has been strong on pressing her preacher-prophet-pastors to hold our elected officials accountable.

David respected "thus saith the LORD" because in spite of his sins, he loved the LORD. He respected Yahweh's prophets and prophecy for another good reason: David was also a prophet (Acts 2:29-31). When Nathan walked in and told him the story of a sinful man guilty of high crimes against a family, David delivered a scathing verdict; David found out that his verdict was for him. Immediately he humbled himself before the LORD, repented, and received the LORD's punishment and mercy.

Twice in his life King David raised the ire of Yahweh. Twice in his life, he humbled himself and received the LORD's punishment and pardon (2 Samuel 12 and 1 Chronicles 21; the latter passage is also told in 2 Samuel 24). David was a man after God's own heart (see 1 Samuel 13:14). We must pray that those who lead us in our nation are people after God's own heart.

We must never be ashamed to pray that our prophets will have the ear of the King. We must pray our prophets are like Moses.

Moses wished for the day when all of God's people are prophets (Numbers 11:29). And we must pray that the prophets who speak from our pulpits will address/denounce sin in whatever form it occurs, but also provide God's remedy for salvation through our Lord Jesus Christ.

### Concluding Thoughts

Our worship in the African American church may be different, but not so different that many of our white brothers and sisters have not benefited greatly from our worship styles. Many have now allowed more expressive worship styles in their congregations that lift the spirits of their people. Things may be changing, but there is still a great deal that needs to be accomplished.

Our worship has self-help elements in it that serve as a catharsis of liberation from any type of disenfranchisement experienced in the workplace, in domestic domiciles, in the marketplace, and sometimes, when we hold political office in places of government. Our counterparts often hold us under strong scrutiny that results from a suspicion that suggests black people will not make the grade and succeed in public life.

Sometimes that suspicion is spelled out in the workplace with such clarity that if it were not for the blessings of our celebrative worships, complete with songs that glorify God, prayers in Jesus' name that clarify our longing for a closer walk with God. The verbal praises indicate that God Almighty, by His Holy Spirit has come to indwell us and make Christ real to us, we would not survive.

If it were not from the blessings that come from a strong dose of encouragement from prophetic preaching that calls us to see God in His holiness, and that we are to respond to His holiness through responsible Christian living and responsible Christian action, we would sink beneath the load. The stress of negative press would be unbearable, were it not for the voice of the prophet in the black pulpit and the black church showing us God's love moving us forward, comforting us, and helping us through all of these things we call tough situations. Thank God, His prophets have a right to speak. Preach on!

* This was written April 1, 2008 before Senator Obama was elected 44th President of the United States of America. It was entitled "The Prophet Is Right (Wright)." The title is changed for use in this document. **Senator Obama's speech entitled "A More Perfect Union" was delivered after these lines were written.

# Chapter Seven
## The President Is A Man and Not Our Messiah

American Presidents influence legislation and changes in public policy and the introduction of new documents that may later become law. The Congress passes them as Bills that are signed into law by the President. America does not need Messiahs and Saviors; we need Presidents. President Obama was wrongly thought to be the long-awaited Messiah of black people, white people, brown people, red people, yellow people; but he is not nor will be messiah, but the man we elected to help make a change in our system of doing things the same old way in Washington DC, a reality.

Some have tagged him as a Socialist. I mentioned Dinesh D'Souza at the beginning of this work. He posits that Obama knows little of the sufferings of black Americans, because he is the product of a biracial, new kind of American, with Kansas and Kenya birth origin, that reveal from both his matrilineal and patrilineal descent, he is perhaps (my thinking here) a person of privilege because Obama, unlike most African Americans, has no "Bill of Sale" in his background. Again, with regard to Socialism, Obama, according to D'Souza, like his father before him – who in Kenya was exposed to the harsh rule of colonialism – is reacting against European and American aggression on the colonialist side. According to D'Souza, President Obama may be exhibiting tendencies against capitalism and war.[23]

President Obama is not a socialist but a realist and believer in a fair capitalism and how it works in the free enterprise system where the rich do not step on the backs of the poor and the middle class with oppressive economic tactics that break them and keep them down. Maybe this is the side of our president that remains to be seen by some. Such need to see President Obama is for America, not against us. Maybe what blinds them is their own rage and desire for power.

D'Souza may be trying to resurrect a question mark about the reality that our president is a Christian, a born again believer in the Lord Jesus Christ. It also suggests that President Obama is a contradiction to Christianity. Thank God, it did not keep the Electoral College from going with the will of the American majority.

One of the greatest mistakes that many Americans make is trying to paint any president as a messiah.

---

[23] Christian Broadcasting Network, *700 Club Iinterview*, October 7, 2010 – viewed and listened to by author.

It was of interest that I read a note regarding President Obama's book *Obama In His Own Words*, written while he was the Senator from Illinois, with Lisa Rogak (Editor). The note said Barack Obama, "has been hailed as the clear savior of not only the Democratic Party, but of the integrity of American politics."

The problem with this is, saviors and messiahs become disappointments when they cannot transform a whole world or area around them to the liking of all that have dubbed them with that *title of distinction*. In all instances, messiahs and saviors that are crafted in the image of humanity, made by humanity can be lifted and removed by the very people who put them in these perched positions, all too swiftly with severe impunity when they are taken down, by those who created them.

Barack Obama has never conceived of himself or deluded himself with the idea that he could save America, the Democratic Party, or American politics. He has tried to influence American politics with a positive message that "change does not come from the top down, but from the bottom up." He is working overtime trying to inspire a lackluster Democratic Party that needs his influence, to raise their sights, and to see the need to accomplish better things for the American economy and the people who are hurting most from our economic woes. During THE 2010 Campaign, President Obama asked the Democratic Party to step up to the plate of responsibility.

According to Cynthia Tucker, Atlanta Journal – Constitution columnist who rarely bites her tongue on any subject, but "tells it like it is," says, that President Obama has a human flaw. She said in a recent article, "Amplified by the right-wing message machine, Republicans paint President Barack Obama as an unyielding left-winger, an unreconstructed liberal who refuses to compromise. The president's critics have turned the truth inside out: *One of Obama's greatest political weaknesses has been his stubborn, and unrequited love for bipartisanship*[24] *(italics mine, added for emphasis)."*

That alone would disqualify the president from messiah/savior status. Messiahs and saviors of human making would never stoop to bring consensus and bipartisan cooperation. Messiahs and saviors (our Lord Jesus Christ excluded) operate on how much fear they can generate to get their point across. Obama automatically fails to fill messiah shoes; thank God.

---

[24] Cynthia Tucker, "Obama's Grand Ol' Misstep," *Atlanta Journal Constitution*. Sunday October 17, 2010, p. A24.

Some African Americans feel he has rebuffed them. President Obama is trying to reach across a wide chasm and be the president of all Americans. Obama did not turn out to be the messiah they were looking for. These are misplaced values and hopes.

He has "ruffled some feathers" in Washington D. C. He tried to influence the legislative agenda so that those who are at ease in Zion, will feel a sense of woe if they do not craft and support legislation that reaches out to middle America; legislation that says, we have not forgotten you are without a steady paycheck, your home is being foreclosed on, and your family's living condition is intolerable. Those "ruffled feathers," as they are called, have fired back in ingratitude and an election of a Republican majority in the House of Representatives, who called the recent election, a referendum on Obama's presidency. They would never be able to get away with that with a messiah, and survive politically.

Our President is not nor wants to be a messiah or savior, but the chief executive of this nation, leading by influencing that which is both objective and reasonable, by dealing with what he inherited, when he came into office.

Let me share with you a little about what I know about President Obama. When I became the 18th President of the Progressive National Baptist Convention, Inc., headquartered in Washington D. C., in 2006, one of the first things the General Secretary Dr. Tyrone S. Pitts (now retired) did, was to arrange for me to accompany Dr. Marian Wright-Edelman, fearless leader of the Children's Defense Fund to a meeting on "the Hill" in the Senate building, to talk about issues of children's health care. We were privileged to talk to then Senator Hillary Clinton and Senator Barak Obama.

I had the opportunity to meet with Joshua DuBois, who was one of his staff members and now Director of the White House Faith Based and Neighborhood Partnerships. Joshua was enthusiastic about he and I and Dr. Pitts meeting together and told us he was seeking support for the Senator's run for office, as leader of our nation. We did not get to talk with Senator Obama at that time, but he showed up at the meeting with Dr. Wright-Edelman.

The senator gave us a warm handshake, looked us in the eye and spoke with much hope on a comprehensive health care plan that would rectify some of the inequities in the system that kept our nation's poor children from having adequate health care.

Senator Clinton was equally enthusiastic about talking to those accompanying Dr. Wright-Edelman, promising to do all she could to influence the process for passage of comprehensive health care coverage for our nation's nine million children who were *health care defenseless* – my words. I left that meeting with a prayerful hope that Mr. Obama, the Senator from Illinois, would be our first African American President. I told Dr. Pitts my sentiments.

As the Campaign hopefuls began to rev up their political engines in 2007, moving around the country to key areas where they wanted to secure the Democratic and Republican nomination of their respective Parties, Senator Obama came to Atlanta to speak at a rally at Georgia Tech.

Here in Atlanta, he met with a number of the African American Faith Leaders in Atlanta; in our midst was our sainted Dr. Joseph Echols Lowery, President Emeritus of the Southern Christian Leadership Conference who prayed the Closing Prayer at the Presidential Inauguration Ceremony. I felt blessed to be among them. I went over to shake the senator's hand and tell him where we met. I did not want to assume that he remembered me.

He said, "I know who you are. Let me tell you how I know you…" I thought, okay, another politician. His remarks to me were truthful, warm and personal, sharing with me his Easter Dinner with a pastor friend of mine, and the pastor's direction for Senator Obama to get in touch with me. He spoke to each of our Faith Leaders, some he had known across the years, and others with whom he was willing to get to know.

We all spoke to Senator Obama, openly and candidly about our hopes for the future, and what it would mean to have a man of integrity who was concerned for America's hopeless, underserved, underfed, to run for President of the United States. We were looking for someone who understood Americans with low incomes, lack of health care, jobs being shipped out of the country, educational opportunities being given to the rich and famous, were suffering. We talked about other domestic and foreign policy subject matter.

We shared, that it was of the utmost importance to us as Faith and Community Leaders in the African American South to join with other Faith and Community Leaders across the country in the belief that the person in the White House would use the power of the Oval Office to help struggling America. We believed Barack Obama could make that difference.

He assured us of his genuine empathetic concern and willingness to work for change, and if, he had our support, we would see a difference.

He then went out to Rally and spoke of the need for change in America. It was there that he made the impassioned words "turn the page" come to life. He invited us to come along and support him and help him "turn the page" on political apathy, doing business as usual.

He spoke persuasively, helping us believe that every American can make a difference, with the words, "yes we can," punctuated by our chanting, "Yes we can," with our applause and cheers. I was determined from that point on to support his candidacy.

Later at a meeting of Progressive National Baptists in our Leadership Conference of December 2008 in Washington D. C., D. Paul Monteiro and Joshua DuBois shared with our pastors and officers present that I was one of the first of the African American Baptist leaders to publicly share my support for Senator Obama, President-elect Obama. In some places I spoke (as a private citizen), I felt no shame in supporting Senator Obama. I still feel I supported and voted for the right choice, the right man; not a messiah or savior – I already have that in Jesus Christ our Lord – but a man who was running on a campaign for change with support from the bottom up.

Since that time President Obama has met with and talked to African American and Evangelical faith leaders on several occasions.

## Chapter Eight
## God and Government, Religion and Politics

One of the problems that often cloud the political picture and focus on a steady agenda for the American people is the intrusion of religion and politics. There are definite advantages, to discussing some issues in light of their constitutionality. For example there will probably always be a lively debate around what Freedom of Religion means.[25]   However when we allow the religion of one group to overshadow the belief system of another group, it becomes politics – right vs. left, which party Jesus endorses, etc. Isn't God supposed to be Partisan?

In America, one's religion is one's belief in God and the right to worship God in his or her own way. In the past, when my own foreparents and most of the American frontier people forward, spoke of religion it was spoken in the same vein of what we call *accepting Christ as our Savior, being saved, being born again.* The prevailing meaning still refers to Christianity, and in a broader sense, other religions of the world.

However the word *Religion*, especially in America today, might not mean the same thing. Use of the word can become a means of imposing one's belief on another, and using it to label the domination of one group having political advantages.

Most evangelicals tend to talk about Christianity (knowing that it is one of the major religions of the world) as being a relationship with Christianity; religion being a set of rules. Some people get uptight about the subject of religion and how it seems right wing conservatism (I would say, extremisms here) has dominated the political scene with its not-so moral, moral messages. Whether conservative or liberal, both Democrats and Republicans are guilty of sinning and being immoral where ethics in government are concerned.

It would be nice if moral men (and women) were ethical examples in government, all the time. But that just is not so. The problem is universal, politicians like anyone else are human, and they must be the first to see they too have flaws.

Talk of religion and which group has the most pull and influence on earth in politics has its drawbacks.

---

[25] See Ken Paulson's article entitled "Church, State and the First Amendment: What O'Donnell Needs To Know" October 19, 2010, on the First Amendment Center Online web site. O'Donnell, a Republican from Delaware ran against and lost to Democratic opponent Chris Coons for the United States Senate seat.

There is one subject among many things, that some people will not object to, and I suspect a larger majority than we know, is a whole discussion around God and government. For Christians, regardless of denomination, God ordained government for good. It proceeds from the idea that there must be orderliness in society. God has always had people in government who worked for the good of the nation.

In the days of Israel, Moses, then Joshua, Samson, Deborah and Barak, David and Solomon, Esther, Nehemiah, Daniel and the three Hebrew men, Hezekiah, etc., all served the purposes of God: serving God meant governing with His interests in mind and the needs of the people of Israel, in mind.

The New Testament record is less obvious where government involvement of the pious is concerned, because the Herods, Pilate, and the Sanhedrin tainted so much of religious and political life in Jerusalem. I suspect that this is what I am referring to here in this chapter as religion and politics. In religion and politics, both the governing authorities and religious rulers can and will conspire and cooperate to get rid of anyone who threatens the status quo.

It was religion and politics that killed Jesus. It was our God who governs from glory that overturned religion and politics and raised our Lord Jesus Christ from the dead (see Acts 3-4). It was religion that ruled against Christianity and sat silently by as Herod killed James the brother of John in Acts 12. It was God Almighty who sent an angel, overruled politics and religion, governed on His terms, and delivered Peter from being executed in like manner.

Religion and politics kept African Americans in slavery, bondage and poverty after slavery, Jim Crow and the segregated system of caste and class, and the forced denial of their voting rights, until God and government in the Dr. M. L. King, Jr., Presidents J. F. Kennedy and L. B. Johnson Era pushed for desegregation of schools, civil rights and voting rights, and housing desegregation in the 1960s.

In our own not-too-distant history, religion and politics helped Adolph Hitler kill six million Jews. Many apologies from nations of the world have been given to Jews whose families survived the death camps of Germany (**Auschwitz, Sobibor, and Treblinka) whose** religious leaders complied with the rule of silence. They stood by while Hitler had a field day. Where were God and government when all of this was happening, we asked? He was in the mouth and writings of the German Confessing Church that was jailed, because they opposed Hitler and considered God's will more powerful than religion and politics, openly condemning Hitler's overt and covert actions.

God was working in government people with a conscience, underground, behind Hitler's back, helping to destroy what Hitler put in motion.

Jesus settles a controversy by advocating that we render to God what is His and to Caesar what is his – which means we pay taxes to government (see Matthew 22: 15-22).

If Jesus sees the role of government in a positive light, with Him in authority with His Father God Almighty, then His people should see government in its proper light. Government is utilitarian, that is to say, hopefully for the good, in the United States, "of the people, for the people, and by the people."

For another thing, we should not assume that government greed is the way of God and that piety and patriotism are synonymous. God never sanctions greed. He condemns it. The blending of piety and patriotism were perhaps, Jonah's problem, his piety and patriotism were confused and it bled over into intense nationalism. Often piety and patriotism mishandled, makes those who promote it, blind to many truths that are violated where humanity's ills are concerned.

Paul speaks well of some in the Roman government, *those in Caesar's household.* In fact Paul and Peter both take the stance that we are to understand that God ordained government and as His people, we are to give government their due. Of course, persecution can come, but we are assured that God will show us the good from it. That good for Americans comes in the second paragraph of our Declaration of Independence, which provides that government can be refashioned if need be, by the people. In America, her citizens are given the right of dissent. It says, *"That whenever any Form of Government becomes destructive of these ends, it is the Right of the People to alter or to abolish it, and to institute new Government..."* That should help us forever keep government honest.

The Old Testament speaks of prophets who stood apart from government to keep it honest. It was Samuel, Nathan, and Gad; again, Daniel, Jeremiah, and Ezekiel to name a few, stand out, as personalities that helped government stay honest. The Chronicler writes in a pronounced way of God's judgment on Uzziah's decision to trump the temple priests and play God. It cost him his throne and his life.

It was, according to Isaiah, in the year of Uzziah's expiration date with life, that he (Isaiah) *"saw the LORD, high and lifted up"* (Isaiah 6:1-8) in the temple environs, which made him bemoan his own sinfulness and succumb to divine cleansing.

Afterward, Isaiah received his commission when he surrendered to Yahweh, and said *"here am I, send me."*

God and government need not be antithetical to each other. Government can be viewed in a positive light in our homes, schools and churches. We should, I would say, raise our children to have a healthy respect for government as an instrument of God for the good, and train them to take positions of responsibility in government as salt and light in the world, and as a way of keeping culture on track.

It is religion and politics that more than a little poses the problem. We all know how slavery was endorsed by religion and politics, and how some denominations in the Christian faith parted company and formed their own base of denominational operations. We all know how desegregation and voting were opposed by organized religion before and during the Civil Rights Movement. Dr. King talks about it in his book *Strides Toward Freedom*.

Religious conservatism in its most extreme presentation takes advantage of political situations and turns it to its advantage. It has used misguided preachers to propagate political unrest. There are times according to Scripture and from life, religion and politics comes with propaganda and payment, and does what the late Dr. William Augustus Jones, Jr., said, turns "prophets into puppets."

Amos condemns the puppets of Bethel who prophesied falsely. Jeremiah was clear in Jeremiah 29: 8-9 that prophets of the people, were clearly not of God and preached a message of deception. He warned them not to fall for that. *"For thus says the LORD of hosts, the God of Israel: Do not let your prophets and your diviners who are in your midst "deceive you, nor listen to your dreams which you cause to be dreams. For they prophesy falsely to you in My name; I have not sent them, says the LORD.'"* These prophets, paid by the ruling political system to preach a politically correct message rather than the truth, were political pawns.

I cannot help but assume that we probably have some profiteers in prophets' robes that would just as soon be "paid puppets" of the political system rather than to speak for God and trust Him for provision. I do not speak specifically of anyone in particular, but simply lift this point for the sake of thought.

Preacher, scholar and seminary Professor Dr. Obrey M. Hendricks lays out the fact that Ann Coulter went so far as to use the subject and cloak of religion as a way to emit a message that liberals were against Christ.

He lays out how Newt Gingrich was able to manipulate Republican sentiments to become totally "anti-Democratic Party" in the media, with catch phrases that would construe the truth as different from what the liberals called it.

With enough confusion, Gingrich was able to keep conservatism free from the mainstream media's grasp of the truth, no matter how much truth existed in the Democratic Party.[26]

My point here is to suggest that religion and politics have often crawled into the bed of agreement together (figuratively speaking), to perpetuate a system of abuse, remain silent on vital issues that affect the public good; have robbed and raped the poor and middle class and then pocketed the tax gains and reapplied them to suit their own evil intent. Religion and politics as others say, make strange bedfellows.

God in the hearts of those who lead and legislate and interpret law government are heard vehemently decrying one race dominating and subordinating another, one sect over another, and do their best to work for the good of the governed. All political disagreement is not corrupt. But we must guard against political philosophies becoming the State-ordained religion. Instead, we must allow God to bring government into compliance with His will: the establishment of "just" laws that work for the highest good of all who are the governed. Amen.

---

[26] Obrey M. Hendricks, *The Politics of Jesus*. (New York: Doubleday, 2006) pp 258-259. See Coulters statements, "Liberals hate America"... "Liberals hate all religions except Islam."

## Chapter Nine
## Respect and Civility In Attitude and Speech

Never before in my lifetime, have I heard such terrible talk broadcasted on the television, radios and across the Internet in the name of Free Speech (perhaps it was different in times before me). Free Speech as a constitutional safeguard according to my remembrance of the Free Speech Amendment, respects a person's right to his or her opinion on a subject, but does not entertain a person's right to be discourteous and disrespectful of those to whom they refer.

It seems that our politicians, some incumbents, and some opposing the incumbents, can only campaign on negative speech instead of real issues; they campaign on character assassinations, while others, stir negative public sentiments with language that is vitriolic and vile. And we call that Free Speech. Nowhere else is this more truer than during the Tea Party's efforts to bring down the Obama Administration with people in the streets portraying the President as a villain in many of their public parades and public meetings.

Others, a pastor Rev. Steven L. Anderson in Arizona, a Baptist Pastor no less, who needed attention, called out "I hate Obama..." and went on to say how he was asking God to do away with this President. One pastor who was a vice president of the Southern Baptist Convention and continues to have a go to "court" passion to prove the president is not an American citizen, Rev. Wiley Drake, "has prayed for Obama's death," RNS reported back in 2009.

The Southern Baptist Convention is a convention of Baptists that advocate the verbal inspiration of the Scriptures, and call for adherence to Scripture in the lives of its members. Scripture does not condone hate; it is just the opposite – love your enemies. Why make the President the enemy? What type of example does this set for children and youth, whom we want to respect us, but then notice that we disrespect others? We do ourselves a great disservice with our hate talk, so called. We set a poor example.

We have also watched in horror (it was horrifying to me at least) as former Governor Sarah Palin on her talks in Nevada, on Monday October 18, 2010 came near "cussing" but didn't cuss, by saying something that others would applaud and defend in the name of old fashioned politics and supporting your favorite candidate. She moves along with her "gosh darn," language that is definitely from my perspective, as dangerously "left of decency" in political talk as one can be.

Sarah Palin openly threatened the Republican Party on the news interview that day, while signing autographs for her enamored followers who shouted "run for president" with polite thanks from her lips. She said, "if the Republicans don't straighten up, you are finished." She was hailed by the news as "the Darling of the Tea Party." God help us if that is what being "darling" means. When you are in the public eye, though not perfect, the first thing a politician should remember is how they are cast in the media. They should care about how they are perceived through their use of the English language. Media can help or hurt you.

We can't forget, by looking at how Conway and Rand from Kentucky showed their disdain for each other, leaving their debate podium without shaking hands. When did all of this start? Better yet, when will it stop? Media feeds us what we want.

Some in the American public thrive on being vile in speech. We have pushed the "decency envelop" to open the idea that being moderate in conversation is out of style in American politics, and definitely out of the picture in public debates. There seems to be a certain type of *dumbing down* of decency and courtesy in speech. There is even a certain type of discourteousness in addressing one's political opponent; Conway and Rand are the classic example. I call it bad manners.

Who can forget the Vice Presidential Debates of 2008 when then Governor Sarah Palin, snidely said to then Senator Joe Biden, "May I call you Joe?" That was the closest, perhaps not the first time, that I saw how easy it is to be politely disrespectful of another's office in the name of "friendly" political debate. Our thoughts can also go progressively from right wing extremism to what has often been tagged as leftist immorality.

Let's pull off the gloves of decency and "get it on!" "Get it on in the media" has by every standard of indecency, encouraged language that degrades rather than language that uplifts. This is especially true in the arena where political debate before elections is concerned.

If we do not demand decency in debate and promise to vote against the candidate who most reflects denigration of other human beings – Democratic, Republican, or Independent – media will show us whatever keeps their ratings up. Media allows it, because there is no moral outcry against it. Media understands dollars and cents from their sponsors, not decency and sense, in many of our television and radio station corporate offices.

And, if there is a moral base supporting decency and respect in political debates, and wholesome television programming, decency must be proven by the amount of dollars that can be poured into stopping indecency. If there are not enough dollars of decency to impose decency, the dollars of indecency win out. We have to demand decency in speech and demeanor, or have the debate (and indecent programming) pulled on the spot. If we turn off our televisions, silence our radios, and close down our Internets, the media can tell when John and Suzy Q. Public are not watching; the sponsors also get the message.

Decency in debate is what I am promoting and talking about here. There has always been disagreement about government. There will always be disagreement about government: its size, its influence or intrusion into private and public life; too much control, not enough control; all are subjects that candidates differ on. Fine.

The point is to debate your differences not your bad language, bad behavior, and being downright nasty in front of the cameras in hopes of raising your ratings at the polls. Whatever happened to examination of a candidate's record in office, or the challenger's record of public service or lack of it, and a clear understanding of one's qualifications as being good for office and the American people? We definitely need to rethink this.

The Constitution of the United States of America is clear on who can be our President of America: **the American best qualified**. It has always been our understanding that the person running for office of President, according to **Article II of the United States Constitution**, Section 1: **President and Vice President**, Clause 5: **Qualifications for Office**, there three things and three things only that qualify any America who wants to become the President and Vice President of the United States: (1) those persons must be a natural born citizen of the United States; (2) they are to be at least 35 years old; (3) inhabitants of the United States at least fourteen years (there is an assumption that the President and Vice President respectively, shall be of sound body and mind).

Religion, education, race, economics do not enter the picture when it comes to being our nation's president. We, however, hope our presidents, presidential and vice presidential hopefuls who candidate for office, are reasonably educated. It is also equally clear that the rest of our other government branches can be filled with qualified people. It does not say they have to be rich or poor, just qualified. But political debate between two candidates for the same government office usually begins and ends with character assassinations.

It thrives on disrespect for the one person running against the other person for office. Clearly, this has to do with television; the channel with the most people watching gets the ratings, and the speeches have nothing at all to do with the issues that should be debated.

Being a Christian, Scripture demands I be respectful of those in office and not speak evil of dignitaries – see 2 Peter 2:10-22 (especially verses four through ten) and Jude verses 8-13 (Jude is only one chapter). Both writers are closely aligned in their language on maligning those who are in office.

President Obama observed correctly in his Press Conference on Wednesday, November 3, 2010, one day after the Midterm Election, regarding political bickering, "And with so much at stake, what the American people don't want from us, especially here in Washington, is to spend the next two years refighting the political battles of the last two…" He went on to tell of a personal moment when talking to a small business owner in Richmond, VA about the small business owner's concern for American political differences and politicians who debate these differences, returning to "civility in our discourse…"

The president said, "I do believe there is hope for civility. I do believe there's hope for progress"… we are "a nation that's overcome war and depression, that has been made more perfect in our struggle for individual rights and individual freedoms" (quotes are taken from the White House Office of the Press Secretary – Press Release – dated November 3, 2010).

Thank God, President Obama and many other incumbents and opponents are not thinned-skinned. I hope they all will continue to work to create decency in speech when debating, and civility in their dealing with each other. It just might set the tone for civility and decency in speech in public and in private as we talk to each other, and as Dr. Joseph Lowery and others would say, "not at each other."

## Chapter Ten
## Our President Needs Our Prayers

I enjoy the fact that both Jeremiah the prophet and the Apostle Paul are in tune with the Holy Spirit. They both encourage us. No, they command us to pray for government. First, Jeremiah says it this way, with regard to Judah during their exile in Babylon. *"Thus saith the LORD...And seek the peace of the city hither I have caused you to be carried away captives, and **pray unto the LORD for it;** for in the peace thereof shall ye have peace." – Jeremiah 29:7 – KJV.*

Now, the Apostle Paul to Timothy: *"I exhort therefore, that, first of all, supplications, prayers, intercessions, and giving of thanks, be made for all men; for kings, and for all that are in authority; that we may lead a quiet and peaceable life in all godliness and honesty. For this is good and acceptable in the sight of God our Savior; who will have all men to be saved, and come unto the knowledge of truth" – 1 Timothy 2:1-4.* I will not argue with those who may not believe Paul wrote this, but someone else. We are free to disagree with respect to each other's opinions.

The point, however, is the call to prayer that is issued here by both Jeremiah and Paul for those who lead us. This then becomes a point that must become the spiritual posture of at least the Church and hopefully for a nation that says since we are a *(one) nation under God*, we recognize prayer is in order for those who lead our government. We should be prayerful then, in a positive way, for those who lead us.

Now with that said, we must pray for President Obama and all other presidents who succeed him in office. He needs our prayers. I have heard him say in Town Hall meetings, where someone from the crowd, not Rep. Joe Wilson's negative comments (State of the Union Address – January 2010), but someone positive saying, "We're praying for you, Mr. President." And he has graciously said, "You know I believe in prayer...I can use a lot of prayer..."

Our president is a man of prayer. He has submitted to the prayers of those in the faith community when he was on the Presidential Election Campaign Trail. He has gladly received prayer across the board from the faith community on issues that are critical to the welfare and safety of our nation. I was a part of the African American Clergy leaders who met with President Obama for brief times of prayer. President Obama is a man of strong faith in God and the belief that prayer is necessary to his making good decisions that will bless our nation.

Let us pray. Let us pray for President Obama and all of our elected and appointed officials. Prayer is an essential part of the Christian DNA. It would be helpful for prayer to be a practice of our national attitude. It must become a priority for all whom, as our elders used to say, in prayer and covenant meetings, *know the worth of prayer, pray for me.* Let us pray.

Praying to God and then doing His will, not just reading and quoting His Word (reading and quoting is good and necessary, especially so, when it is in context), will be key to the survival of *any* nation as a people whose faith traditions reflect the Judeo-Christian ethic of being fair as well as being faithful in government. The Psalmist said, *"Blessed is the nation whose God is the LORD..."* Psalm 33:12).

When we pray for God's kingdom to come, as Jesus taught us in the Model Prayer (see Matthew 6: 9-13 and Luke 11: 1-4), we are asking God Almighty to rule over us on earth, as He rules over everything in heaven, with us carrying out His will on earth; it is His will that has been established in heaven. This is reason enough for us to pray for our president, the Congress, the Supreme Court, and government at the state, county, and municipal levels; no department is to be left out. With this being said then, our president needs our prayers, if, for no other reason than that he is the moral leader of the free world.

We should be praying that President Obama leads the nation with wisdom and understanding. We should be praying that those around him would be wise advisors. They may not be Christian, but God can use them to do His will.

It is amazing what can happen when the nation prays for her leaders. Moral rectitude without hypocrisy can be established when we earnestly pray for the President and our elected officials of the United States of America. We should be praying for their safety and security and the safety and well being of their families. We would do well to pray for bipartisan cooperation and agreement on things that will bless our nation.

We should pray for our president as Commander-in-Chief of our Armed Forces; that they are never recklessly sent into harm's way to fight a personal war that pleases a political party's greed, but that we will always send our troops to places where our allies genuinely need our help, and to places that will thwart terrorism and will keep America safe.

Decisions to draw down troops from Iraq required prayer, and we pray for the citizens of Iraq that they will be able to sustain themselves with the peacekeeping forces that remain behind to help them transition.

We must pray now, because President Obama has set a time line for troop withdrawal from Afghanistan. There are some people who like war because they like to fight. Fight terrorism we must, at home and abroad, but war for war's sake is not profitable. The President needs our prayers to prioritize, along with the wise counsel of his Armed Forces Chiefs what is best for our Troops, for our economy – war is costly – and what is good for American interests.

It is easy to be critical when you do not occupy the seat of influence that any American president occupies to guide the affairs of state. We can sit on the sidelines and say what President Obama and others presidents of America should not do (should not have done – where past presidents are concerned, and judged by historians), but the truth of the matter is, we do not have that responsibility. Our responsibility is to pray for them.

It is always reported that with the late President Harry S. Truman, he made sure America and Congress understood "the buck stops here."

The president is responsible for guiding the nation, and this President amidst the stormy torrents of those angry that he is making a difference, needs our prayers.

## Chapter Eleven
## A Few Words On Being Conservative Or Liberal

I remember when being conservative meant fiscal responsibility and being liberal meant being generous. Both words also meant being morally responsible for yourself and looking out for your neighbor.

Being conservative in spiritual things means and meant that one is an adherent of living out the Scriptures, and being liberal in the Judeo-Christian tradition means "doing justly, loving mercy, and walking humbly with your God" as Micah the Prophet said we should (Micah 6:8). These words are not wasted.

There is a sense that conservatism in our theology, as Obrey Hendricks put it, refers to our adherence to the Scriptures if any are proclaiming to be followers of Christ. Scripture informs our morality. We often say that the Bible is an all-sufficient guide for matters of faith and practice. Faith being what we believe and practice is what we do with what we believe. Our being conservative in the faith of Christ and obeying the Scriptures, with the leadership of the Holy Spirit does not necessarily conflict with our political beliefs as Christians. No Christian buys into everything their Party says.

Conservative used to mean not being wasteful; while exercising excessive liberality could be checked by common sense decisions which did not border on extravagance. This is still true in some circles.

However, when it comes to the political life of America, we are talking about something that has a different tone to it. Being a Conservative, as I understand it, has to do with maintenance of the status quo. Being a Liberal means, too much advancement of the masses, too fast, at the expense of government.

It is necessary to remind us that conservatism and liberalism in what follows, is a political philosophy. In our society, being conservative has often been switched to be the regulation of morality of the right-wing conservatives, while being liberal has often been identified as the bulwark of left-wing immorality.

These two explanations above in the previous paragraph are a "way of life" which generally does not touch true politics, although these explanations often bleed over into politics as truth.

**Conservatives define themselves** by saying, being conservative in government is belief in limited government, individual responsibility, and the free flow of capitalism (unchecked, mind you). Many want to make money for the sake of making money, not for what money can do for our sagging economy.

**Liberals define themselves as** being for individuals and the masses. They support affirmative action, expansion of the workforce, human rights issues conservatives will not touch; education reform, social justice issues, are part of liberal dialogue. One website I visited describes **a political conservative** as,

> "A person who favors decentralization of political power and disfavors activist foreign policy."[27] It then goes on to define **a political liberal as,** "A person who favors individual voting rights, human and civil rights, individual gun-rights, laissez-faire markets, and the gold standard. Favoring ideas that treat all people with equal justice regardless of educational, financial, sexual or racial status.[28]

Frank E. Smith wrote, "Naturally, the liberal politician to who I normally refer, is one who is definable as a liberal by his scope of American government in helping to broaden the traditional American opportunity for all American citizens to improve their "life, liberty, and the pursuit of happiness"[29]

Liberals are not limited to the Democratic Party any more than Conservatives are sole members of the Republican Party. They come from every region of the American political landscape. It is interesting that Smith above shows how thinking can be segmented to one type of liberal from a region of the country. "Whatever our definition of liberal, both history and common usage have already written a definition that irrevocably links the term "Southern liberal to race.""[30]

The Republican Party, however, boasts itself as Conservative in both their agenda of limited government and gradual (slow) change, while the Democrats often boast themselves as Liberals with a belief in equal treatment under the law and government control in the affairs of the nation.

Let me mention one illustration of differences in political liberalism and political conservatism.

---

[27] English Dictionary at www.AllWords.com .

[28] Ibid.

[29] Samuel DuBois Cook, (Ed.). Frank E. Smith, "Liberal Leadership in the Present-Day South," in *Benjamin E. Mays, His Life, Contributions, and Legacy*, p.291.

[30] Smith, 291.

Liberals believe in gun control and conservatives support an almost unrestrained abuse of the gun control laws, in spite of the violence, they see in our streets, in the name of the right to bear arms from the Constitution. I do not classify this as Constitutionalism, as some in the Conservative wing would describe it; it is more so, in my opinion, a failure to regulate disregard for human life. Then the shoes change feet. Liberals support the woman's right to an abortion, while the conservatives preach right to life. Both may permit limited abortion under extreme conditions; say, rape.

In the chapter where I discuss race, I mentioned a group of Republicans who call themselves *Frederick Douglass Republicans*. They say, among other things, they are not conservative. Perhaps they bear the other title, Moderates. But their belief is very closely aligned with Republican thinking: limited government, respect for Constitutional life, and what Conservatives call individualism.

Liberals and Conservatives believe in good government. It is not limited to Democrats and Republicans. According to Obrey Hendricks' quote of Robert Kuttner, "Liberals and Conservatives, agree, in principle, about the value of liberty. But where liberals differ is their insistence that liberty requires greater equality than our society now generates."[31]

It is interesting to note that the greatest good for the public good has resulted from the leadership of liberals. The strength of conservatives has been their wide-awake vigil for the promotion of limited government, though they will broaden things when it is to their advantage.

The United States presidents that have been tagged liberal are identified as such, because of their concern for the equality of opportunities being opened to the masses rather than the rich minority. It is no small matter. It has been testified with historical documentation, that America's liberal presidents in both parties have widened the margin for public success. Hendricks lists George Washington's speech and says that George Washington was a liberal.[32]

Of course this does not rule out the fact that Presidents George Washington, Thomas Jefferson, and Andrew Jackson, who were all called liberals, all owned slaves.

---

[31] Hendricks, p.294.
[32] Hendricks, p. 293.

In terms of their slave holdings it was the tenor and tone of the time that equality was not extended to black people whose vote did not count and were determined to only be three-fifths human.

According to Howard Zinn, "The liberal notion of history, however, was a limited one, for it asserted that the history of the Negro in America has been determined by slavery and segregation…Thus, from the beginning of our national history, it was established that the attitude of government toward the Negro would reflect the degree of libertarianism in other regards – for liberty is easily divided into compartments"[33]

Zinn sites American presidents "Thomas Jefferson, Andrew Jackson, Woodrow Wilson, and Theodore Roosevelt are all part of the American liberal tradition…"[34]

Even Lincoln, although acting out of expediency freed the slaves through the signing of the Emancipation Proclamation, is called liberal, because of his action. He was doing what he had to, to preserve the Union. His doing what he had to; moved beyond the ebb and flow of conservative thinking at that time in history.

Again, the greatest gains have come when liberals in the presidency and Congress have moved beyond limited conservative thinking to reach the majority of America's poor and working class citizens, choosing to advance their opportunities for economic empowerment, job security, retirement, medical benefits, and the right of Unions to protest and negotiate for fair wages. Conservative thinking seems to stick with keeping the poor, poor, and allowing them to work themselves out of poverty, by "pulling up" their own bootstraps. Liberals give them boots.

President Theodore Roosevelt through his liberalization of government brought us the Square Deal. His distant cousin Franklin Delano Roosevelt during his presidency brought us the New Deal. I believe that President Barack Obama is bringing us "The Good Deal." He is considered a liberal.

But the work he and the Congress have done to benefit Americans thus far have represented closing the gap on Americans not being able to have the basic benefits that have always been the mark of a reasonable existence: Health Care Reform, rebuilding the Infrastructure – this means many jobless will have jobs.

---

[33] Cook, Howard Zinn article "American Liberalism: Source of Negro Radicalism" in *Benjamin E. Mays, His Life, Contributions, and Legacy*, pp. 340-341.
[34] Ibid, p. 345.

We will have the introduction of fair business regulations where excesses at the top shared some of our country's biggest names who inspired a financial meltdown on Wall Street will be halted; tuition upgrades in the arena of education for students of middle class parents are available to be taken advantage of. This is a "Good Deal."

It is also true that many conservatives in the Democratic and Republican Parties may not know this "Good Deal" because they have been tainted by bad deal politics. For example, when the Stimulus money was sent out to the States from the Federal government, many of the governors of the Republican conservative right refused to accept the money, or took it and doled it out to their favorite people, without it ever doing the good it was supposed to do to reach the masses for the common good. My own State governor refused it publicly.

If being liberal then means, and it does mean looking out for the least of the left out, in politics as typified in the Democratic Party, we need to know a "Good Deal." Good deals are not regularly seen; we need to know one when we see it. We need to "drop the rage, turn the page," and give thanks for President Obama **at least trying** to do what he promised when he was vying for the votes of the American majority.

Is this what I am choosing to call the "Good Deal" perfect? Of course not, nothing in life is perfect. We know it is not perfect in either political quarter, because some in both parties try to derail everything before they look to see what needs work. This is however, the best we have had in recent years; we are finally looking at poor Americans, Middle Americans, underserved Americans, and taking action to help them rise above levels of poverty and joblessness in our country.

The recent Midterm Election of November 2, 2010 has shown a Republican and Tea Party victory in the House of Representatives of the United States Congress, with John Boehner as the new Speaker of the House; and Mitch McConnell, the Minority Leader of the Senate who had promised in earlier News interviews prior to the elections that President Obama would be a "one term president" (October 23, 2010).

However, on ABC News in an interview, Representative Boehner was not so quick to embrace Senator McConnell's statement; in fact Boehner said, "That is his (McConnell's) desire." When News Anchor Diane Sawyer asked Rep. Boehner about going to the White House to eat with President Obama and how he felt toward President Obama referring to him, on the campaign trail this fall; Boehner told her he holds no personal grudge against the President.

Representative Boehner also indicated President Obama's references to him (and his for President Obama) on the campaign trail was "just politics"; and nothing more. If that is true, and we will withhold judgment here, then there might be civility on issues – we will watch and see. The Senate, however, is still under the Control of the Democrats. This signals either a political stalemate where stubbornness in the House or retaliation in the Senate will be the order of the day, and show itself in the not-too-distant future.

The President has vowed to work with the Republicans, in his speech the day after Midterm Elections comments on November 3, 2010 at the White House Press Conference. He is open to any new ideas that will "bless" (my words) the American people. It will more than likely result in tax compromises, and it will mean a better flow of feeling and good will between government and business. At the Press Conference, President Obama told the Press and the nation, on Wednesday, November 3, 2010, the day after the election, that he wanted businesses to know that he was not against them, but wanted them to flourish.

This is a deliberate attempt on our president's part to reach out to the Republican Party, also identified as political conservatives. While the President is more of a Centrist, as I see it, he represents the Democratic Party, which may also be classified as liberal. President Obama's reaching out and the Republicans, I hope listening, will not be all bad.

We will watch to see, if tensions will die between the two parties, and whether the GOP will try to dismantle everything that has been done to help the American people. Being conservative or liberal is a choice; in this case, a political choice, just as it is being Democrat, Republican, or Tea Party. However, the choices made have consequences for our elected officials. Their job is to serve the common good, work for the common good, and through bipartisanship, give us a healthy and economically stable America.

No one will be angry about who serves in which party of either house, so long as they serve their country with a spirit that says, Conservative or Liberal, we are about the business of a better America. That is what will count most: the business of America. Which political philosophy one chooses will not count as heavily as "what happens to America's will"; although we know that the philosophy of being Conservative or Liberal could well be dropped in favor of American interests, instead of Party interests.

## Chapter Twelve
## America Needs To Turn The Page and Repent!

I have talked about dropping all of this rage that has been played up in the media as essential to the political survival of conservatism and liberalism. Perhaps, now it is time to talk about Repentance. In Scripture, repentance always precedes a spiritual revival. *Metanoia* in the Greek speaks of repentance in a manner that suggests active engagement; it is a turning from something to something. In this instance, it means turning from sin to God Almighty.

Wherever there has been national repentance in history, spiritual revival comes. When spiritual revival comes, there is an outpouring of doing what is right about the poor, and those who are disenfranchised by monopoly politics. Morality springs forth and affects the nation. When those in authority in Scripture have called for repentance, God blessed the nation.

It would do us well to look at this prayer prayed by Rev. Dr. K. Gerone Free as he talks to God about mean-spirited people in America needing to change their attitudes. He follows it with what I believe to be prophetic insight into our times and the remedy for our sinfulness.

He uses 1 Timothy 2:1-4 as the basis of his prayer. *Therefore I exhort first of all that supplications, prayers, intercessions, and giving of thanks be made for all men, 2 for kings and all who are in authority, that we may lead a quiet and peaceable life in all godliness and reverence. 3 For this is good and acceptable in the sight of God our Savior* – NKJV. Below is Dr. Free's written prayer and prophecy.

### His Written prayer

"Father God, I pray for my country. LORD, America is in great turmoil and unless we send forth men and women who are compassionate toward others our nation will suffer greatly. Father, I pray for a miracle that will change the hearts of people to vote against those who carry such hatred toward our President, for this is not pleasing to You. LORD, many do not know that this election will determine Your favor upon us or Your judgment against us. Father, I pray that those who speak against those who speak for the have-nots and left out of this nation will not rise to power. LORD send forth voters and workers who will stand for righteousness for all. In the name of the LORD Jesus Christ I pray. Amen."

## The Prophecy

"God has said that if America elects men and women who speak hatred and malice against those who seek to help those without health care and vital essentials for daily living then this nation will come under serious judgment. The nation needs to know that God is not pleased with our behavior over the last two years and that God placed President Obama in office so that America might see how far they are from true righteousness. This nation will truly see destruction if men and women of hatred are placed in positions of leadership across this land." This is what God keeps speaking into my spirit.""[35]

This of course may not fully play itself out until after the Midterm Elections of 2010, but it will surely be worth watching, as we think about the fact that the next Presidential Election will be 2012. I do believe firmly, that we should pray, without malice toward any in public office, that those who have been elected will not be a "majority of the haves," who legislate against "the have-nots" among the American people.

One may ask, will this come true, if we don't repent? The Scriptures teach us that if a prophecy is of God it will come true. If it is not, then we do not have to worry about it.

Here is what Moses had to say about it as he spoke Yahweh's desires for Israel. Deuteronomy 18: 21-22 says this; *You may say to yourselves, "How can we know when a message has not been spoken by the LORD?" If what a prophet proclaims in the name of the LORD does not take place or come true, that is a message the LORD has not spoken. That prophet has spoken presumptuously. Do not be afraid of him.* (NIV).

Again, the Word of God stands firm - *The voice said, "Cry out!" And he said, "What shall I cry?" "All flesh is grass, and all its loveliness is like the flower of the field. The grass withers, the flower fades, because the breath of the LORD blows upon it; surely the people are grass. The grass withers, the flower fades, but the word of our God stands forever."* Isaiah 40:6-8 (NKJ).

Finally, the words of Paul to Timothy are helpful and instructive to those who claim to be steeped in Christian conservatism and are so-called in public office.

---

[35] The Prayer was sent out on Friday October 15, 2010 across the Internet to many of his prayer partners. He has granted me permission to use this in its entirety for this manuscript. It is very timely in any election period where America is concerned, and should be broadly applied to Democrats, Republicans, Independents, and Tea Party members, as well as the American public...

In 2 Timothy 2:19 we find these words, *"Nevertheless the foundation of God standeth sure, having this seal, The Lord knoweth them that are his. And, Let every one that nameth the name of Christ depart from iniquity."* (KJV). I feel this prophecy is bipartisan in its outlook. You may disagree with my views, and this is perfectly acceptable to me. I am also of the opinion that there are many others to whom the LORD has spoken in this regard.

Nor does this prophecy imply a Democratic or Republican victory in Congress; that is up to the American people turning out to vote in any election. This election cycle included what resulted in gains for the Republican Party being in control of the House of Representative and the Democrats in control in the Senate: both houses are called "the Congress." What it does suggest, is that, it is time to turn the page on behavior that is less-than-acceptable in God's sight and start a new chapter of life. Such a turning, crosses party lines, and is not negative toward any particular group except mean people who think hatred is an everyday occurrence; and they are doing God a favor by hating.

When anyone turns the page in a book, it is to read the rest of the chapter, start a new chapter, or it is an indication you have come, to the end of the book. In life, when we turn the page, we usually turn the page on a bad past, bad memory, bad practices, and have made the determination that we will start fresh with good behavior, looking for quality, decency, and respect in our relationships.

Turning the page might even mean getting new employment, moving up in our present employment. Let's turn the page. It may also indicate: new income streams, better government, run by people with a good conscience in all their decision-making: Democrats AND Republicans.

Repentance precedes renewal; renewal means revival. It is time we take a good look at ourselves, "drop the rage", repent, and "turn the page" by turning to God Almighty.

Someone will ask, "Of what do we need to repent?" For one thing, we need to repent of our anger and rage that we are still a nation untrusting of ethnic minorities. We should repent of the fact that when we are given a blessing or blessings, we curse ourselves for having to receive it – ie., President Obama.

We need to repent that we are angry about health care, having been signed into law, looking at the cost, rather than looking at the benefits.

We need to repent that our governors in some states, still want State's rights to outweigh federal laws, which make accessibility to affordable health care an issue; which they want paraded before the Supreme Court in order to find a way to legally throw us back into higher premiums and denial of health care benefits, because of pre-existing conditions.

We need to repent before God that we look to discredit reform without ever considering that without some reforms, business and industry would get away with murder (figuratively speaking).

We need to go before God Almighty and repent for those banks which are so eager to foreclose on people who cannot pay, and will not, in some states, allow debtors "due process." We should repent that we have expanded "the due process clause" to protect big business, and negatively affect those for whom the Fourteenth Amendment was written to protect.

Because of haste and the lack of "due process", people can be evicted on short notice. We should repent that some of our nation's poor were put into mortgages by some banks that knew they couldn't pay, but with the help of realtors, who made a good buck, some banks knew they could get their houses back and resell them again for profit, when the mortgage customers were evicted, did it anyway; all of this in the name of "the American dream" of home ownership. Foreclosures turned into the American nightmare for many.

We should repent that we are enraged by the fact that Congress helped reform credit card company practices. With high interest rates, and people having no jobs, Credit Card debt is the new Share Cropping System of the old South. The rates are so high that much like the Sharecroppers of old, who every year, as my great grandfather was told "Boy, you like to near about got out of debt"; you never do under an oppressive high interest rate system. It was then and now, a debt that is difficult to pay.

We should repent that America is a debtor nation.

We should repent for our schools that are still not up to standard in many of our nation's urban school districts, and that we allow ourselves to rage against improvement of our educational systems. We have, as one person put it, no one is demanding and telling the students they must succeed – this is a generalization, of course. We want God to bless America, when America does not always want to bless herself.

We should repent that we spend billions on everything, but our nation's poor. Dealing with the poor and global poverty and trying to be responsible abut climate changes are social justice issues, from which there can be no rest. Along with getting people saved from sin, we need to see to them being fed, clothed, and taken care of.

God calls us in Isaiah 1:16-17 *"Wash yourselves, make yourselves clean; remove the evil of your deeds from My sight. Cease to do evil, Learn to do good; seek justice, reprove the ruthless; defend the orphan, plead for the widow"* (NAS); and throughout the book of Isaiah these are matters that call for our involvement in social justice issues and warn us for our lack of concern when we may try to ignore them, but should not. Consider God's message through Isaiah in the following chapters: 3:15; 11:4-5; 28:5-8; 32:16-18; 41:17-20; 56:1; 58: 1-9, or Matthew 6:19-21; Timothy 6:1-19; 1 John 3:16-19.

Who can escape the call to social justice in Amos 5: 10-15, *"They hate the one who rebukes in the gate, and they abhor the one who speaks uprightly. Therefore, because you tread down the poor and take grain taxes from him, though you have built houses of hewn stone, yet you shall not dwell in them; you have planted pleasant vineyards, but you shall not drink wine from them. For I know your manifold transgressions and your mighty sins. Afflicting the just and taking bribes; Diverting the poor from justice at the gate. Therefore the prudent keep silent at that time, for it is an evil time. Seek good and not evil, that you may live; so the LORD God of hosts will be with you, as you have spoken. Hate evil, love good; establish justice in the gate. It may be that the LORD God of hosts will be gracious to the remnant of Joseph"*(NKJ).

Or that same chapter, verses 22-24, which offers rebuke and encouragement, *"I hate, I despise your feast days, and I do not savor your sacred assemblies. Though you offer Me burnt offerings and your grain offerings, I will not accept them, nor will I regard your fattened peace offerings. Take away from Me the noise of your songs, for I will not hear the melody of your stringed instruments. But let justice run down like water, and righteousness like a mighty stream.(NKJ)*
Not only is repentance called for but action after repentance and correction.

We need to repent that there are homeless people on our streets and government ignores them, and will not house them. James 1:26-27 *"If anyone among you thinks he is religious, and does not bridle his tongue but deceives his own heart, this one's religion is useless.*

*Pure and undefiled religion before God and the Father is this: to visit orphans and widows in their trouble, and to keep oneself unspotted from the world... "* (NKJ).

James 2:5-8 says, *Listen, my beloved brethren: Has God not chosen the poor of this world to be rich in faith and heirs of the kingdom which He promised to those who love Him? But you have dishonored the poor man. Do not the rich oppress you and drag you into the courts?*
*Do they not blaspheme that noble name by which you are called? If you really fulfill the royal law according to the Scripture, "You shall love your neighbor as yourself," you do well... "*

Consider James 2:15-16 *"If a brother or sister is naked and destitute of daily food, and one of you says to them, "Depart in peace, be warmed and filled," but you do not give them the things which are needed for the body, what does it profit?"* (NKJ).

We should repent that little children in many cases are left alone at home, to raise themselves, because their parents are struggling to make ends meet and must work two jobs, destroying family unity and family cohesiveness.

We cannot escape these social justice issues that follow either. We should repent that we have not condemned gang activity, which our youth see played out in the news from adult gangs; our children are being cut down on the streets, and also being aborted. We are killers of our own children. The devil is in these details: if there are no children around, then the message of Christ will be lost in culture. Because once all the adults are dead, there will be no children to evangelize. We need to get the devil out of here and save our children.

According to Psalm 127:3, *Children are a gift from the LORD; they are a real blessing* – (TEV). Children bring glory to God and promote the human heritage. People who don't love children have selfish spirits.

I also believe, we are due to repent for the way we have been *poor stewards of the earth* (italics for emphasis) – also referred to as Environmental Justice. We have raped it, poked holes in the atmosphere, and spend more time in space than we do helping our citizens. I cannot prove this, but I will say it from a point of personal observation. Every time we go into space, there are some strange and stormy changes in our weather.

Those changes reduce homes to rubble, and cause insurance rates to increase. Those storms cause trees to fall on power lines and food is wasted, because refrigeration and electricity are imperiled, and the city, county and state workers do not have enough people or equipment to keep the power going and turn the lights back on to the peoples' satisfaction and feelings of safety and security.

These storms cause basements to flood, and new flood planes have to be rethought, redrawn, and redefined, because old definitions are proving wrong. Where flooding was not an issue in times past, it now is an issue.

God made it clear, we were to be fruitful and multiply, subdue the earth (Genesis 1:28); in Noah and his family's case, repopulate it (9:1). I am not one to be anti-scientific where discovery is concerned. I thank God for scientific discovery and what it does to benefit the improvement of heath care, finding new sources of renewable energy, etc. However, I also recognized that the LORD has not indicated nor implied anything with regard to "subduing outer space" – remember Babel (Genesis 11:1-9). This could be a warning to us, all in terms of being overly ambitious about what we "think" we need to discover, as opposed to the so many unexplored phenomena here on planet earth that will profit humanity.

We should repent that we would allow ourselves the luxury of hatred of any people, rather than helping all the people that we can help. There is a definite need for repentance. Repentance changes us, makes us feel better about ourselves, and regulates our hearts to be more benevolent toward those who most need it, and forgive those who are too ignorant to accept our help when it is given. Let's repent and "turn the page" to progress and human development.

## Chapter Thirteen
## Beyond the Rage and Turn The Page

When we repent, we are willing to embrace change, "turn the page" on our lives, and grow. God is still calling us to repentance, so that He can provide revival and healing in our land. *"If My people who are called by My name will humble themselves, and pray and seek My face, and turn from their wicked ways, then I will hear from heaven, and will forgive their sin and heal their land"* – 2 Chronicles 7:14 (NKJ).

Rage will make you sick, if you nurse it too long. Some of us are sick, because we carry far too many grudges in our hearts toward others. We need healing. Healing turns the page on our rage and makes us whole.

We would do well to become more prayerful in our attitudes, speech, and actions. Prayer will not kill us, prayer will bless us. In prayer, we earnestly learn that God should have complete control over our affairs, with our willingness to humble ourselves. As we often say in worship, "Let us pray."

We should think seriously about for what to pray. We should be praying for our nation. Pray that our spirituality will inform our morality; that the moral imperative will govern and that we will behave like children of God, even though everyone in our world has not come to Christ. Christians can still pray for all to be saved. That is when true revival engulfs our nation, and our priorities change from selfishness to selflessness, and we become willing to learn that we must be brotherly and sisterly toward all, who do not share the same faith in God that we share.

It might be through our repentance, praying, and renewal, the nation will be renewed to study war no more in our streets, in our corporate offices; no more war in our family circles, leaving them for greener pastures. We can pray for immorality to be curbed. Revival is needed.

David Spitz shows us our weaknesses when he says, "For instance, surely we did not need the Kinsey reports to tell us that marital infidelity and what we are pleased to call sexual aberrations are widespread. Nor do we require the more sensational revelations of our newspapers to know that lawyers and businessmen are often guilty of tax evasion, price fixing, embezzlement, and food and drug violations and anti-violations, and any number of other white-collar crimes. "[36]

Revival is needed as the spiritual method of turning our rage into righteous indignation. We can see that drugs, drive-by shootings, and random killings, still plague our streets. At some points in time, our children are almost the endangered species. Drugs are no longer an urban problem, there are drug dealers who have taken over the suburbs of some areas of this country, and our children – white, black, brown and yellow, – are the victims who are now in programs, aimed at getting them off of their high they seek.

These programs are seeking to reduce their heroin dependency – the drug of choice, the news is reporting, because it is cheaper than the pharmaceutical drugs which they crave. With sensible programs that will help dry/clean them out without drying their brains, we have hope and the need to study war no more; take rage and turn it against drug addiction in a positive format. We need to study war, no more. We need to "turn the page". Revival is needed.

No more war with our neighbors, because we can clearly see that their needs can be assessed and met with eyes and hearts of compassion. Praying will help us have a listening ear to the Spirit of God, who will be directing us to engage social justice issues, as they are and confront them and work to solve them.

It is a sin for toxic waste dumps and treatment plants to be built in areas where minorities live, and a majority community has enough clout to keep the treatment plants out of their neighborhoods.[37] The majority stays healthy and the minority citizens go into ill health and have medical bills they cannot pay, due to their low-income status. If the devil is in the details, then we need to have enough spiritual power through prayer and cooperation with God and each other, to "get the devil out" and lock the door on him (Ephesians 4:24-27). Prayer helps us to go beyond the rage and turn the page to the chapter that records the changing of our ways, and building where no one will be harmed.

Beyond the rage is a brighter day of hope. Beyond the rage and pages of bitterness we must leave behind, is a brighter day where a stronger America counts her blessings and lives what she preaches: democracy.

---

[36] Cook., David Spitz, "Power and Nonviolent Resistance: Thrasymachus and the Politics of Civil Disobedience" in *Benjamin E. Mays His Life, Contributions, and Legacy,* p.261.
[37] One Asian church in Metro Atlanta protested a treatment plants, but was not strong enough to keep a plant of this type from being built next door to its worship facility.

Liberty and justice for all is no accident. America still has potential. Dr. Gardner C. Taylor, the President Emeritus of the Progressive National Baptist Convention, Inc., said on one occasion, America is God's great experiment in democracy. In response to that I believe that God does not intend for the experiment to fail; He is expecting us to work on it!

We still have potential. We can still "turn the page" in time to experience genuine revival and realize our brightest and best hopes. It may mean looking within ourselves for the answers.

But I believe, with all my heart, it means looking beyond ourselves to the One, who made us and knows our faults and our potential for faith. If God believed in us enough to allow our nation to stand this long, looking for some positive fruit to come forth from our lives, we need to have faith in Him, more so than ever before, because without His favor upon us we fail!

It is true, God has given us free choice, but free choice means disciplining ourselves to make the right choices. Free choices mean living responsible lives as citizens on earth and later as citizens in heaven. Being given free choice does not mean that we can be licentious in our behavior, indecent in our demeanor, or downright inhuman. We must see ourselves better than that and act accordingly. Change in public policy is never a reason for a lack of restraint, because we disagree with the change.

Just as children can't throw off all restraint and have temper tantrums, neither should we. Adults must model restraint and work within the law for changes that are for the good of the whole. Our potential often lies in our being able to accept change when it arrives.

Our flexibility in the matter of change can be the compelling argument, change works! It can be the propelling factor for our upward mobility into the things that matter: "life, liberty and the pursuit of happiness." Our capacity for change enhances responsible actions in our homes, churches, office complexes, shopping centers, and in housing developments where neighborhoods lose the ethnic flavoring that everyone in a particular group was accustomed.

We must go beyond our rage and "turn the page" to that which embraces our potential as a great nation whose trust is in the LORD. Going beyond our rage, is a necessity we cannot bypass. A nation enraged will never "turn the page", never do anything constructive and helpful, but will remain angry for all the wrong reasons.

If we refuse to go beyond our rage, there will be no change in our behavior; it will not matter who is president; when we stop being angry with President Obama, we will only be angry with all the rest of presidents after him, for any reason we can find. That is what happens when we do not check our rage at the door, and "turn the page" to progress instead of impeding progress with our hostilities.

America needs to be as Lincoln said it should be after the Civil War in his second Inaugural Address: a nation "with malice toward none." It may not sound practical with all of the violence we have experienced in our short history, but it is sound advice.

We need to turn our rage into productive methods that will help stop terrorism. We must "turn the page" on our rage and start paginating our future with good will and good intentions; with good behavior, and a legacy of good works that can be left to the generations that come behind us. Like children, we must allow ourselves to be unencumbered with inconsequential matters, and decide like adults, to grow and joyfully reach our full potential.

We must not be like other civilizations that after 200 years suddenly dissipate and go off the scene. History shows us that a people without conscience, and people who continually look only at surviving rather than thriving; a people who slip into patterns that reflect greed, envy, jealousy, rage, will not make it. All such civilizations eventually become history.

We can "turn the page" and become the one country that proves the historians wrong. We can be a greater nation, if we make the conscious decision to allow God to govern our nation. We can become "one nation under God, with liberty and justice for all." That is not an impossible thing to pray for and cooperate with.

As the angel Gabriel said to Mary, *For with God nothing shall be impossible –* Luke 1:37; Mark 10:27. The message rings true for us as well, if we will listen and heed it.

# Chapter Fourteen
## When God Governs

I would like to look closer at the conservative/liberal arguments to see where God fits in. For one thing, I have discovered throughout the Old and New Testaments, when God governs there are discernable patterns of governance that look at what is good for the people; all of the people who will be governed by the LORD and His Son. These discoveries are plain enough for everyone to see, and are not Democratic or Republican, Liberal or Conservative in scope. Those patterns become a modern paradigm for government today in the United States of America.

When we look at this Biblical perspective, there is no such thing as "limited government" from the Republican side of the aisle, where God is concerned, and neither is there such a thing as a bureaucratic bulge from the Democratic side of the aisle, where God Almighty is concerned. God does things in an efficient manner that shows direct involvement in the lives of the voting constituents – Israel voted a great deal, much to their own demise, because they rejected God's involvement in their lives, and experienced forty years of wandering in the wilderness, before entering Canaan as their Promised Land and seventy years in exile in Babylon for their rebellion.

God the Father believes in taking care of the people. His Son, the Lord Jesus Christ believes in taking care of the people. Many call this Liberation Theology. God never portrays Himself as the victim. Even if His people are victimized as Liberation Theology often projects, God is the Mighty Deliverer. God is involved in the affairs of His people. He is the Victor. Let's look at God the Father first and then look at Jesus Christ His only Son.

From Adam and Eve, who ruined it for themselves, when they came into conversation with the serpent, whose political views were totally different from its Creator and influenced their rebellion against divine authority (God had given Adam and Eve the run of Eden, with certain restraints which at the time were quite liberal, in the sense of God's generosity, not as a political philosophy – not too much to ask for in a Garden that watered itself – see the Genesis account in chapters 2-3), God cares for those He rules over.

God showed direct involvement with Moses leading Israel out of bondage from Egypt in direct opposition to the conservative Pharaoh, king of Egypt and his political system. Pharaoh was a conservative. No argument there. He believed in limited "autocracy." The limits were on the people. The law was in his hands.

He let the Hebrews make bricks without straw, demanding that the daily tally of brick-making be up to what it was before the straw was pulled, according to Exodus 5:1-19. Pharaoh tagged the Israelites as lazy, unproductive, and in need of more work to break their welfare mentality, since they wanted a holiday to go and worship the Holy One of Israel. God toppled Pharaoh's government and economy for "non-compliance" with His will and plans for His people Israel.

God Almighty led Israel out of slavery into the wilderness in search of the Promised Land, providing them with the assurance of His Presence with a pillar of Cloud by day, and a pillar of Fire by night (Exodus 13: 20-22). God moved them to the Red Sea in time to cross when the East wind blew, walking Israel over on Dry land (Exodus 14 and Psalm 105:8-12), allowing Pharaoh's army to drown when they got deep enough in the riverbed on the dry land. The water curtains on both sides closed.

And at every turn, even when Israel raged and rebelled, God provided them with everything they needed, including health care coverage, denying it only when they violated the rules of their policy, deliberately deciding to sin as their slave masters had (Exodus 15:26). God gave them a generous Constitution, which today if followed keeps order and morality at the forefront of any society (Exodus 20:1-17).

God supplied their food, while they traveled, did not allow their clothing to wear out, and as Moses said of Asher, gave them shoes of iron and brass (Deuteronomy 32:27 - KJV). When God governs, there is direct involvement in the lives of those He governs.

As I mentioned earlier, the Son of God believes in direct involvement in the lives of the people He governs. Just as His Father received people, any that the Father sends to Him He receives (John 6:37). The conservatives said, Jesus had a devil (Luke 11:14-26), although their own demonic estrangement, cancelled many of their reservations for heaven, it happened because they did not receive God's Son.

These extremists on both sides of the aisle (Pharisees and Sadducees – the right wing and leftists) plotted to kill Jesus at every turn, because He was a threat to their existence with Rome and her political-militaristic machinations (See John 11:47-55). Jesus was much too generous for the Conservatives of His time on earth, which happened to be the governing body for Affairs of State, under Rome and the Herods. Jesus was not a political or religious Conservative or Liberal. He was the Ultimate Change Agent who had come to seek and to save those who were lost.

They instead, did whatever was expedient to advance themselves and to keep Rome happy – they were accommodationists. While the opposition was quick to politicize the situation, Jesus was doing what He does best; doing what His Father did – see John 5:19, 30; 8:38; 10:30; 14:10. Jesus is the Ultimate Agent of Change.

In every case that is recorded in the New Testament, Jesus makes a special effort to be involved in the lives of those He taught. When Jesus allowed His disciples to obtain food from the fields in violation of Sabbath law, He became offensive to those who wanted to argue Law. Jesus refuted them and showed them He was in charge and refused to let anyone go hungry any day of the week including the Sabbath *"Then he said to them, "The Sabbath was made for man, not man for the Sabbath. So the Son of Man is Lord even of the Sabbath"' – Mark 2:27-28(NIV)*.

Jesus' involvement with the lives of people reached into delivering a woman from stoning by the conservatives who "knew Jewish Constitutional and Roman law" (see John 8:1-11), and tried using it against Him to make Him commit religious and political suicide. It did not work. In another situation that went against common thinking, Jesus healed a woman on the Sabbath (Luke 13:11-17), and a man on the Sabbath (Luke 14: 1-6).

The Pharisees and Sadducees were always outraged at His actions, ideas, and verbal teachings. His liberal interpretation of God's will over against their narrow interpretation of God's will was more than they wished to take. They banned together to be sure that Jesus died Roman execution style, without ever accounting for the fact that God would raise Him from the dead (Acts 3:13-14; Romans 8:11).

When the masses followed Him and listened to His teachings, Jesus had compassion on them: providing them with adequate health care coverage, doing operation-restoration of limbs, just for the asking, and providing food for hungry multitudes. The Conservatives in His camp who believed in limited government, with no participation in the lives of their constituency, sounded the alarm that there was no way to feed a multitude; *send them away and let them buy their own food before the markets close* (Matthew 15:15-16).

Their type of reasoning is very close to what we hear today in conservative politics, that wants to strip big government involvement in favor of big business bonuses and a personal prosperity, which leaves the poor to pull themselves up, by their own bootstraps. The Liberals in His apostolic company could not see the logic in investigating the situation to assess what was available for feeding.

They said, with no malcontent intended, when they produced a lad's lunch of two small fishes and five cup-cake sized biscuits, *"what are they among so many?"* (John 6: 9). They wanted Jesus to do the math; that was too small of an amount to feed the multitudes (John 6:5-13). Jesus challenged them to look within their resources, search the situation out and see what they could come up with. Jesus believed in involvement, "you give them something to eat"; He had already told them. Jesus was not being Machiavellian.

And because God governed everything in and about Jesus' life, Jesus took those two fishes and five loaves, prayed and thanked God for what the hungry travelers "were about to receive for the nourishment of their bodies," and had His apostolic group learn some simple management principles about distribution of the goods. The loaves and fish multiplied. Everyone ate, everyone was filled, and no one left hungry. There were, according to the Gospel accounts, twelve baskets full of food left. The disciples didn't need to worry about hunger and starvation.

Jesus taught His followers that for lives to change, involvement in the lives of the underserved is necessary to the well-being of people's quality of life; that when we take care of those who need it most – all the basic necessities for human existence – our involvement is applauded by Him and rewarded by Him in Matthew 25:31-40. That is not really a Democratic or Republican, Conservative or Liberal phenomenon. It is **the Ultimate Agent of Change Jesus Christ the Lord**, telling us, *involvement is the right thing to do* (italics added for emphasis).

However, Jesus warns us that our giving cannot bypass the "weightier matters of the Law," things like justice and mercy. These have to do with social justice and the alleviation of poverty and amelioration of unjust civil and social inequities beyond food and clothing. We need to give and we also have to "do all the right things" that go alongside food distribution, to help the underserved.

Jesus warns that limited involvement and benign neglect of those who suffer and are at the mercy of the merciless can be costly, as well as condemning to those who have more than adequate resources to spare, and refuse to share the wealth. It plainly overlooks *"the least of these"* in Matthew 25:41-46. For Christians of course, this is no less than an active faith. *Faith without works is dead*, the Apostle James tells us in his ethical treatise in the New Testament (James 2:12-26).

As God speaks His mind through those who wrote the Scriptures, you can fully visualize where God is involved in the lives of those He governs.

God is calling out to us demanding our involvement with the "least of these" through those He allows to govern. Whether we are a Democrat or Republican or Independent; whether Liberal or Conservative, God calls us to involvement. God is always involved and wants government to do the right thing for the governed.

The Church becomes the reflection of her Lord and Savior Jesus Christ in Acts, when as one reads the ending verses of chapter two, and the ending verses of chapter four, that no one among those gathered together after Pentecost, and the days following, went hungry; they shared their possessions so that everyone who had a need was covered. Paul's message to the church in Galatia was "take care of the household of faith" first, and then reach out to others, who are in need (Galatians 6:10).

There is a principle here, which can be applied to satisfying global poverty and that poverty includes hunger. When the Church leads the way in sharing, everyone can be fed. This means that there would have to be an ingathering of food resources, distributed through our various mission entities, as a combined ministry.

No one would have to go hungry and everyone would be fed. Crops could be grown, agriculture uplifted once again, with seed sowing and planting being done by the local residents, from the supplies given. When their crops grow, they can eat, but in the meantime, we supply them with food until they are able to do for themselves.

It cannot be a one-time effort; it has to be ongoing. The results: God would graciously multiply.

This might be a bitter pill for some Conservatives to swallow, but the Church actually models how true liberalism (generosity) works to help the hurting and be fair in seeing to it that everyone has a right to succeed; and have adequate housing, health care coverage, prisoner reformation, food and water, adequate employment here in the good old USA. We do not have to ship everything out of America to foreign markets that promote cheap labor laws and bad business practices etc.; because we want to escape taking care of our own and keep people out of work in America.

There seems to be no support in Scripture for a conservative ritual of individualism (selfishness in withholding the goods from those in need), and for so many political conservatives who claim God as their guide, for their actions in the right wing of the Conservative movement, for an American Agenda.

They need to go back and read the Scriptures of the Judeo-Christian faith, and allow the Holy Spirit to speak to their consciences about this "bootstrap philosophy" that applies to the bare-footed occupants, who are the underserved in society (USA), and then obey the social action called for in Scripture, and give the helpless some boots! Jesus never skirted social justice issues!

Equal blame can be laid at the feet of Liberals, who feel compelled to campaign on the promise of championing the cause of those left behind by economic reform, racial reform, the solving of housing disparities, but once in office, they side with others in keeping things as they are; only voicing dissent, when their seat is threatened. Some Liberals can be blamed for the rhetoric of people being able to rise, because those particular liberals say, "we are proof that you can succeed."

The idea being, if they have made it, anyone can. This may sound good in their ears, but it does not play out in reality. These same liberals will not see to any doors of opportunity being opened for those left out to enter and succeed.

They too, lead you to believe that God wants everyone to succeed. But they never become God's agents for change, opportunity, and fairness, and yes, firmness on issues that could be solved with bipartisan cooperation and support. They are as much at fault as the conservatives they point the finger at, when saying, "We could have done it, if it were not for them."

When God governs, ALL share in the possibilities of fairness and ALL share in the success!

# Chapter Fifteen
## Media Spins and Election Correction

The Presidential Election Campaign, according to Wolf Blitzer of CNN Situation Room, begins the day after the Midterm Elections. Before we go to the future, let's look at the present.

I notice, as I go to the polls to vote in each Primary Presidential and Midterm Elections, there is little said about whose name is placed, "where" on the ballot. There are probably plenty of people who notice it, but have not aired it as an opportunity to advance our voting practices. Who can forget the 2000 Presidential Election and the State of Florida, which had reportedly gone to Al Gore, but all of a sudden to the chagrin of Media, they had to re-cast what they had just broadcasted: that suddenly the State of Florida was undecidedly in favor of George W. Bush? The Supreme Court eventually picked George W. Bush as our 43rd President: the term was "Selected to Office, Not Elected to Office" for his first term.

There are many stories around the "fixing" of the election, with all of its hanging and dangling chads, stories of voter intimidation. Stories covered everything from interference by the local authorities in various municipalities, and long lines of people who never got to cast their preciously earned ballots, to stories that may have really determined who the next president would have been at that time.

Some good lessons were learned from this. Early voting can be a blessing, pay closer attention to the methods used to secure the ballots; make sure no one is intimidated. When voters are intimidated, let it be reported and dealt with immediately. If the Federal Government has to step in, because the State and County won't, then so be it!

Another lesson that should have been observed in the Media, but I do not think much attention was paid, was "don't predict" without actual figures. Some speculation may be inevitable and acceptable. Media should jump in immediately with objective reporting, when there are voting irregularities.

Another case in point comes from our most recent election here, in Georgia, on November 2, 2010. My assumption is that whose name appears where on a voting ballot may largely depend on who is in power – Democrats or Republicans. Let me be more specific. In Georgia, our last gubernatorial election of 2002 made our state a Republican stronghold.

The Republicans turned out en masse to make it happen and make it stick; they are still the majority. So in our Midterm 2010, we were treated to the names of the three candidates running for governor of our fair state according to the top party.

What caught my eye after inserting the voting card, when the screen showed the names of the candidates; they were listed by Party and not alphabetically. Interesting indeed! The name of the Republican hopeful started with a "D" and the name of the Democratic hopeful started with a "B" and the name of the Independent or Libertarian hopeful started with an "M." The name that started with the "M" was properly placed, but the names of the other two candidates gave the "whose name is first" to the Republican gubernatorial candidate.

Now, there is a saying that goes something like this, "whosesoever name people see first on the ballot that is who they vote for." If that is the case, the Republicans had an unchallenged edge. If we list the names alphabetically on the ballot, Democrat comes before Independent, Independent comes before Libertarian, and Libertarian precedes Republican. Barnes comes before Deal, and Mond follows Deal, as it should be. The Republicans were in power.

I began to wonder how many seniors or persons with eye trouble, even with enlarged letters on the screen, voted for the first name "they saw" without realizing who it was, they voted for; simply because the names were not listed alphabetically? I guess we need to monitor it more closely next time, and if the Democrats or Libertarians are in power, see if they do the same thing. Here is a clear reason for taking your time and looking at the Ballot listings.

Here is something else that has consumed some of my attention. The political spin-masters deliberately tilted the election campaigning coverage with their own twists; **"this is going to be," according to them, an automatic "Republican victory."** Media divided the county; we ended up with a Republican led House and a Senate with the Democrats having the majority. It should make you ask the question, "who owns the Media: Mainstream or otherwise? And why would Media have a biased message and not an objective message regarding how the race is being won, not who is "programmed" into the minds of the American public, to be the winner.

And even if it turned out to be true, will the Republican Party do any different from when it took over during the Midterm of the Clinton Administration?

When the Republicans dominated during the Bush Administration, why could they do nothing to stop the financial bleeding, when the politics turned bloody from the effects of the banking industry fallout? Will they bring change now, or take us backward? Back to the 50's maybe. New faces and old ideas: **going backward.**

I like the way one New York Democrat has put it. He said on CNN that "we must not return the keys to the Party (people) who drove us into this mess in the first place (speaking of the economic downturn) – that we have not recovered from."

Car accidents are bad, sometimes they are fatal; at other times those who come out of it, are crippled, paralyzed, or worst yet, lay in a comma with the death angel hovering over their existence. The government of 2000-2008 does not deserve a second opportunity to do what they did the first time: ruin Americans and then place the blame in all the wrong places. We will have to wait to see the real outcome of 2010 elections in the near future.

President Clinton almost became part of a "going backward" report[38] – as the media reported the Florida campaign of Mr. Meek and Mr. Crist. Media spun a story reportedly, that former President Clinton was encouraging Meek to quit the race in Florida so that Crist (the former governor turned Independent) could win (of course Meek was black and that strengthened the theory that a black can't win).

It turns out, that the rumor came from the Crist camp. Southern conservatism may not be limited to the Republicans across the national network; Democrats (Dixiecrats) may still be alive. I am happy to know that President Clinton was not a part of this backdoor, backhanded affair. It is unfortunate that his name had to be attached to it.

But then, that is how rage starts in negative politics, and if those doing the raging can make it stick, without being exposed, that is what will happen.

Media should be the servant of the public when broadcasting the news. Tell it like it is, with the results in front of them, plain as the nose on their faces, not like someone wants it to look. Media should be helpful with information sharing and not information scaring.

---

[38] Some people will never forget President Clinton's unfortunate remark, "is this some kind of fairy tale, can't win, philosophy?" spoken during his wife's presidential campaign in South Carolina in 2007. Wanting his wife to win was his main issue. Many blacks and whites shared their disappointments, because it seemed to them he believed no black man could win the presidency of the United States of America. He apologized and was forgiven: many Americans hold President William Jefferson Clinton in high esteem, including this author.

Allow me to move away from the election and on to just daily reporting.

With as much as is happening with regard to Osama Bin Ladin not being captured,[39] terrorists setting traps, *it would be helpful not to give so much information away to the terrorists about how the US plans to stop them, what the US knows, etc.* Let the terrorists remain in suspense about our capabilities and quit feeding them information that could be harmful to the American people.

Report that their plot did not work, was discovered or uncovered, and they did not succeed. Show who was captured and they are being brought to justice; that foils terrorist plans.

Do not tell terrorists what and how we plan to stop them. Keep the enemy guessing and at bay. Do not tell them their explosives fall woefully short of being up-to-date. Just let them know that what they did was ineffective and stopped before further devastation could be done. It is usually a shock to the enemy's system when the enemy realizes you out-smarted her or him. Let some things remain a shock and just catch them; and let the element of surprise work against them and in our favor and the favor of our allies.

Do not show maps of where Military Intelligence is setting up. We could be risking putting our troops or villagers cooperating with our troops in harm's way. Keep the enemy guessing! You get the picture. In wartime or peace time, keep the enemy guessing!

It really is how you spin the story in the media. Put a positive spin on it, even if it has a negative outcome. How you report something determines its reception and response from your given audience: when it's negative, find the positive angle or lesson we can learn, and also report that. Whatever you may be reporting in the media: race, politics, religion, elections, violence – even violence has the positive lesson of "don't be violent, it leads to bad results" – report it as a sense of hope and the audience will live in hope.

---

[39] After this manuscript was completed, Osama Bin Laden was killed May 2, 2011 by United States special military forces.

## Chapter Sixteen
## Changing Our Direction For The Future

It is time now to "quit politicking in rage," since the election is now over and we must return to work, looking to see what will take place in the future from those we have just elected, and look at how much public power is resident in the voting constituency called the population. The points below will focus on where we must use our power as a point of privilege to speak as Americans; to issues that must change our direction in this country. I wish to end this book by talking about the future direction our country might want to go. This will necessitate speaking to several issues that we must not escape.

### Work Force Conditions

The Chilean Miners being rescued from deep beneath the earth is a global wakeup call to governments to be more aware and concerned about the safety of those who work in our mines. It is a call for the United States to put more into the safety of those who dig, rather than to have their widows and children, watching as cemetery workers dig an early grave for their husbands and children.

It is very little comfort after an explosion to say, "I'm sorry and our company valued your husband Joe Blow," because the mine sustained an explosion or the mine caved in and everyone suffocated to death. The word **"Sorry" just can't replace a life.** Neither can dollars bring back the voice and presence of someone you have lived with for most of your adult life, and raised a family with them, looking forward to a future that includes retirement, not "black lung disease."

This, perhaps may not be a moral issue to some, because when you are bankrolling dollars and your profit margin is the only thing worth your attention, it is easy to see your workers as expendable. We must look at who runs our Mines (their Mines) and ask them to consider safety measures that show care and concern for the longevity of the work force and not their expendability.

There must be enough of a public outcry that government will go in and regulate (only if the measures are not taken) and Congress pass laws for the safety of Public Workers and Privately owned Mine shafts that make money for the boss, but ignore the Boss's loyal workforce that dig for the coal (gold), that powers the nation's economy. Factories must be retrofitted for the future. If municipalities require upgrades of old wiring in housing, then it must be equally attentive to enforcing that in the factories that are in our vicinities.

There is a need for the "greening of America" as sound stewardship of the environment. Dr. Gerald L. Durley, a pastor and public health advocate here in Atlanta, is one of the foremost spokesmen for Environmental Justice. His preachments and lectures should cause concern for the worker. If there is anger or rage over cancerous conditions that send our poor to the hospitals that cannot find a cure; because the economics won't add up, then channel that rage into demanding better working and environmental conditions.

For that fact, allow me to focus even more closely on this business of how we treat our workers. Treat them with dignity and respect: health, retirement participation, and life insurance (death benefits, if needed for burial purposes).
Dignity of the worker ought to be uppermost in the minds of corporate America. And the American public and our American Government have to remind them.

## Poverty Alleviation Conversation

One of the helpful things that came out of the Presidential Election of 2008, when Obama took office, was the Faith Based reorientation and reorganization. President Obama looked at what his predecessor did, and didn't end it, but instead he mended it into something more in line with 21$^{st}$ Century involvement of non-profits (see I can be critical without being caustic).

For some churches during the Bush Administration, Faith Based Programs were analyzed by one person as being a feeding trough where some churches loyal to the Republican Party could get funding for their social programs of seeing to the needs of the disposed. If you were not Republican or at least sympathetic to the GOP, you would have to wait at the end of the line and the poor would go unnoticed through your ministry; if you were depending on the government to help you.

President Obama reshaped it into the Faith Based and Neighborhood Partnerships, where non-profit entities are encouraged to participate in helping the least and left out through forming a separate 501 (c) 3, as it is called; a non-profit unit that can be reviewed and funded with sustainability in mind, and the local church untied from the government as a ward or patron. That allows, which I deal with further down, opportunities for churches to do some good in a way, that promotes the eradication of housing disparities, food distribution, housing starts, education about debt, etc., without the local church jeopardizing its congregation's non-profit designation with the IRS.

We have talked about the poor elsewhere from the standpoint of God and government; and the subject of involvement in the life of the poor as being correct in any generation. What follows in this chapter are a few things that may help us direct our energies against being angry about what government may or may not be doing, to looking at, what we can do ourselves.

There seems to be reluctance on our part to really talk about, and then, do something concrete that has lasting value for the poor. According to scholar and professor Cornel West, Ph. D., "Poverty can be as much a target of rage as degraded identity."[40]The Church is addressing it, even with the tight economical constraints imposed on the offering plates of our local houses of worship, due to unemployed and underemployed members. But we cannot escape the subject of poverty. It is with us, and it has global coverage: people all over the world are experiencing it in some form – severe to moderate proportions.

As the wealthiest nation on earth, so we are told, in an economic downturn, we have the poor among us, and they cannot be hidden from view. Corporate sins and individual debt service without a way to pay back the debt, has brought America to the point of fast becoming one of the largest debtor nations on earth; we have created a scenario in which "the poor among us" are literally, very visible. They are not all on skid row of our urban communities; many have been put out of jobs, through no fault of their own, and are looking for relief. I believe we as Americans can participate in this movement of good, for the good of the country.

Presidential elections, Congressional and State Gubernatorial and General Assembly elections, City and Countywide elections are good opportunities to hold our publicly elected officials' feet to the fire on how they treat the poor. We must let them know in unequivocal terms, if they are not concerned about lack of employment, homelessness, and the devastating affects of community and global poverty: "you are not concerned about having my vote."

We cannot afford to let any party, Conservative or Liberal, Democratic, Republican, or Independent, take our votes for granted.

## Health Care Concerns

I hope the new Health Care Law is one direction we will continue to support, and will speak so loudly, by our vote and our influence that it will not be torn apart and

---

[40] Cornel West, *Race Matters*. (New York: Vintage Books, A Division of Random House, 1993, 1994) p. 150.

ended, because of Republican right-wing rage. As I mentioned in President Clinton's words, when addressing Affirmative Action, "mend it, don't end it." Allow me to speak to one type of example, which could be a means of mending health care.

There needs to be a clause of some sort that does not penalize people who practice faith as their means to healing. This clause would absolve them from having to participate in a mandatory health care system. There would be a caveat that once they opt out; they can re-enter if they should decide to seek it.

Another area of concern is what we can do collectively if health care were repealed; I truly hope that never becomes a possibility. This is only healthy speculation on my part.

The Republicans have preached, "End Obama Care," referring to the new Health Care Law that Congress passed and the President signed. Republicans and Tea Party members have used it as "Obama Scare" to confuse the elderly, or those not fully educated on the benefits of the Health Care Law. If knife cutting comes to Health Care, then churches and other non-profits will have to shore up health care with the opening of free health clinics.

Now, let me move from personal speculating to reality. Health Care is going to still be needed along with the health care law remaining in tact. There are some churches at home and abroad that make health care happen, no matter what the government is doing. This is commendable. The lists of our sick are growing.

What would have happened, if the Republicans had passed the health care bill, as their contribution to society? Conservatives in Congress would have made it look as if, no matter how expensive analysts would calculate, they would have done something that will help America for years to come. It would have been hailed by Democrats as something worthy of our respect, not our rage. And, if there were parts of the health care bill that needed to be fixed, then everyone would work to fix it, as a bipartisan effort, to be a blessing to those who most need health care. That is how it should be!

### Faith Based and Other Non-profit Involvement

Investing in health care is a mission to be sure. There may not be in this economic tough cycle, enough federally funded centers to cover the health disparities.

Churches, Synagogues, and Mosques, and other non-profits may have to enter in and take up the slack.

While in Ghana in 2007, at the Baptist World Alliance, we were blessed to share with one of our member churches; that sponsor their own, church-run health clinic. They saw where there was a special need to open a way for the sick in remote areas to have access to health care through their church.

They opened their clinic for two days to serve those who were infirmed needing care.

At one point at the end of one of the days of servicing the sick, the clinic was opened; the pastor had to close the clinic down, in order to give the medical staff relief. They had just serviced over eight thousand people that day. They wanted the doctors, the nurses and other medical professionals to stay healthy in order to service the sick. They are still doing medical service in a manner that is worthy of becoming a model for US churches to research and emulate, where that type of need and the vision for it is apparent.

The president of our Progressive National Baptist Convention, the Reverend Dr. Carroll A. Baltimore, Sr., hosts a Mission Conference that he has been at the helm directing for a number of years. I was overcome with joy one year when I served as Guest Preacher for the Mission Conference Banquet, at the positive response the medical community provided in giving assistance to the sick at home and overseas. He makes annual pilgrimages to the Philippines and other places where health care is not a high priority.

Many American doctors assist medical staffs in remote villages that need medical attention where human resources are in short supply. These doctors see themselves as part of God's healing team. As such, they see this as their Christian duty to go in teams to places where the need is highest and minister there to the ill, fulfilling the words of Jesus to see about the sick. Haiti is one of the places that these "unsung" heroes of the medical profession go.

Secondly, there is a strong need to address homelessness in America. Families are not living out in tents, because they want to; many are walking the streets carrying all their worldly goods, because they have to.

And everyone homeless is not a Veteran – though it is often portrayed in the news that way. Everyone with a sign "will work for food" is not a shyster, some really mean it.

While driving to City Hall in Atlanta on November 1, 2010, my wife and I caught sight of a march against homelessness. Most of the marchers were males, silent, but carrying poignant signage that spoke loudly to the plight of many heads of households, who cannot hold their heads as high, as they would like because they are out-of-work, no one had mercy on them, now they are homeless.

One of the signs read HAVING A HOME IS A BASIC HUMAN RIGHT. The most glaring object in their march was a casket, carried by able-bodied men, dramatizing death, because some people were left abandoned, and never received housing. Another sign sang out its message in audible (though only a sign) tones that blasted the consciences of Americans who turn their backs. It said, SPEND MORE MONEY ON HOMELESSNESS, AND NOT ON WAR.

One strong bill voted into law by Congress and signed by the president, to end homelessness and spend less on war and bring our troops home (we need to defend our own homeland), we would see homelessness literally wiped out with "the stroke of a pen."

I am the first to admit that homelessness is a problem that churches can become involved in; however, many of the churches are struggling to keep their worship houses open. A great many of their members are out of work, and therefore, have little if anything to give toward this very important mission ministry that Jesus demands that we address. It takes faith to move a mountain, so we will have to "move the mountain", by whittling down our debt as quickly as possible and put our faith into works of righteousness: homelessness; a mountain that can be leveled and disappear.

We can whittle it down by the faith community buying up abandoned homes, calling in families that are homeless to help repair them, and then give the repaired house to them as a reward of their labors, much like the Habitat for Humanity project. I have said in the past, they can buy it for $1.00. But, if they don't have a dollar, sweat equity is invaluable.

It is also a way to form a non-profit that addresses homelessness and abandoned properties (homes) in our neighborhoods.

It is a way to call in contractors on a volunteer basis to repair, or build brand new on a vacant lot; to teach others the building skills and provide jobs for the jobless. Can you imagine the blessing of forming a work team, headed by a volunteer licensed and bonded contractor, who spends a few hours a day doing repair and training eligible workers in the "mechanics of building?"

This includes but is not limited to: plumbing, heating and air conditioning repair and installation; electrical wiring (properly wired), plastering, painting, carpentry. The benefits and blessings are innumerable.

Even beyond this, churches with skilled laborers could pool their resources to form Mission Teams to build and repair homes to house homeless families.

Then, they can travel to New Orleans and all the Gulf Coast states, after that Haiti, Chile, Indonesia, and other areas of the world where nature has wreaked havoc on the land, where the waters have "Tsunami-ized" (*"ized"* – added by me for emphasis) the country, where fires have ravished the earth, and help restore people to their homes. Where there is inadequate insurance in America, the Church can become the insurance that "no one has to be homeless, without the Church seeking a remedy.

In growing up in Chicago, now living in Georgia, I understood that there was always a sense in which the churches there and here in Georgia, took housing as something that was important to human dignity.

I mentioned the late Pastor Louis Boddie feeding the hungry. I did not mention that he was responsible for housing some of those without a place to stay. I spoke of Dr. W. N. Daniel, he along with Dr. William Holmes Borders, Sr., pastor of the Wheat Street Baptist Church in Atlanta GA, now ably pastored by my friend Dr. Michael N. Harris, set the pace in the late 1960's and early 1970's for affordable housing for the people in the lower and middle income brackets. Dr. Borders and Wheat Street sponsored Wheat Street Gardens and Wheat Street Towers, Dr. Daniel and Antioch (Chicago) were proud to sponsor Eden Green.

I know of others, who have done the same, particularly Dr. J. Alfred Smith, Sr., Pastor Emeritus of the Allen Temple Baptist Church. He and Allen Temple had a record for housing development that still stands under the leadership of his son Dr. J. Alfred Smith, Jr. My predecessor at the West Hunter Street Baptist Church in Atlanta, Dr. Ralph David Abernathy and the church sponsored Abernathy Towers (Dr. Toussaint K. Hill, Jr., is now the pastor). They left behind credible legacies that reflect a care for seniors and other persons who need housing development programs that favor those who might be left out of the market.

Jesus was clear, from the Old Testament that, *the poor you will have with you always* (Deuteronomy 15: 7-11). He chided His disciples for their failure to see what Mary was doing for Him had to do with preparation for His burial and was not an interruption of what they could do for the poor.

According to Birch and Rasmussen, any interpretation that twists Jesus' directive and concern about the poor; and tries to make the Lord look selfish, because He commended Mary's pre-burial act of anointing Him with costly oil (John 12: 1-8) is faulty exegesis without merit, where a wider ignoring exists, of what they call the "wider context of the canon."[41]

There may be, in our houses of worship, as in the Johanine Gospel, a preponderance of thievery among those who raise questions about doing good for the poor as a moral obligation of the Church of God and other people of the faith community, and have no love for the poor themselves. It's worth checking out.

The faith movement must gain momentum. How we treat the poor is of utmost importance to our integrity as the "household of faith."

The poor among us ought to be a first priority within the walls of our congregations (I call your attention once more to Galatians 6:10), and then, we can go to those on the outside.

### A Vision For Those With HIV/AIDS

My long time friend and childhood comrade, Rev. D. L. Jackson, the son of the late Rev. Dr. A. Patterson Jackson, succeeded his father A. P. Jackson, as the pastor of the illustrious Liberty Baptist Church in Chicago, IL in 1994. Pastor A. P. Jackson was known for his social support and involvement in the Civil Rights Movement with Dr. Martin Luther King, Jr. "Pastor A. P." and Liberty also sponsored a high rise for seniors and persons that were physically challenged. It still stands today as a tribute to his leadership; right next door to the church complex. His father before him, Dr. D. Z. Jackson and Liberty had church sponsored housing during his tenure. Liberty has always been a church where the needs of the underprivileged are always a priority.

---

[41] Bruce C. Birch and Larry L. Rasmussen, *Bible And Ethics In The Christian Life* (Minneapolis: Augsburg Publishing House, 1976) pp. 176-177. See their entire chapter on "Making Biblical Resources Available."

At a time when it was not fashionable to talk about, let alone befriend Acquired Immune Deficiency Syndrome people, Pastor D. L. Jackson and Liberty entered into an agreement to form a 501 (c) 3, called the Interfaith Housing Development Corporation and build a home for HIV/AIDS single mothers, so that their children could visit them. The house is called Vision House. It opened in 1997, ready to serve HIV/AIDS single women, mothers and their children. It is state of the art and spells, home. The Chicago Sun Times wrote a whole spread on the faith venture.

Pastor Jackson saw that praying, faith and working are complimentary to each other. Vision House stands as a monument to the faith and vision of a pastor and his people participating to make life more tolerable to those who needed the church's ministry of comfort. Pastor D. L. Jackson and Liberty are to be commended for their forthright involvement with the literal "left out."

Dr. J. Alfred Smith, Sr., mentioned above and Allen Temple sponsored housing for HIV/AIDS persons and members, as a ministry of the congregation. This church's influence has taken the stigma out of the disease, and housed the people suffering in comfortable quarters, without feeling quarantined from public life. Treatment and care go hand-in-hand.

Dr. Pernessa Seal, founder CEO of the Balm in Gilead is another advocate that has had a very strong impact on health and wellness in the lives of the African Diaspora and a special focus HIV/AIDS awareness and treatment.
Her Christian perspective on what we must do about the sick, does not stop with her organization. She partners with faith groups and others in helping to minister to HIV/AIDS patients, and provide a balanced perspective of what faith and medicine and loving care can do, to help improve the quality of a patient's life suffering from HIV/AIDS here in America, Africa, and other global centers where HIV/AIDS need addressing.

These are just a few examples of what people are doing, some are physically off the scene, but their ministry influence is carried on through those who have succeeded them. I do not believe everyone has to do the same ministry. There may be other dimensions of HIV/AIDS and health emphases that determine where a church ministry can be a blessing and most effective.

There are other ministries out here where churches can carve their niche in life as ministry agents of our Lord Jesus Christ. I want to mention a few I am familiar with in the Metro Atlanta Area.

Dr. Cameron Alexander, Pastor of the Antioch Baptist Church (North) here in Atlanta has moved social ministries to a strong level with a full-scaled operation that ministers to people in need of employment, help for those who have drug addictions, and many other ministries that reflect the mind of a pastor and church serving their community. Rev. A. A. W. Motley and the Lindsay Street Baptist Church have greatly improved the perspective of neighborhood development with the English Avenue Community Development Corporation.

Dr. William Flippin, Sr. of the Greater Piney Grove Baptist Church in Atlanta and his three sons (the Reverends William, Jr., Richard, Joseph), Rev. D. Earl Bryant and Friendship Community Church in College Park, and Rev. Anthony J. McMichael and Mt. Nebo Baptist Church (Thomasville) give new meaning to community involvement with clothing for the needy, computer literacy, Family Life Centers; Dr. Cleopatrick Lacy and the Mount Zion Baptist Church in Griffin, GA operates their after school emphases. Dr. Arthur Carson of Springfield Baptist Church reads to Elementary School students as an extension of his ministry.

Dr. Joseph L. Roberts, Pastor Emeritus and Ebenezer Baptist Church where the King's pastored (now pastored by Dr. Raphael Warnock) have opened their church to programs that cater to Senior Care. They are also ministering to former offenders, and working to prevent "at risk" youngsters from being in the prison population pool. Dr. Orlando K. Winters and Mt. Moriah Baptist Church sponsors the Samaritan House; the church purchases food and then gives away groceries to those in need, and once a month, sponsors a hot meal. The examples above, speak to the Church's involvement in social action and social justice ministries.

While these are personal friends and associates in pastoral ministry, my point is not to be biased, I am sure there are many other pastors and churches who are doing these things and more, and I do not know about them. Those I mention in this chapter are practical examples of the things I am addressing.

There are educational programs where churches can become strong and effective in as their ministry objective, after school programs, senior programs, and youth related employment programs; there are multitudes of opportunities that exist for those who will hear the LORD speak by His Spirit to their hearts. My point is the Church community has to be active in the lives of our communities, blessing our communities with our social activism; making every effort to heal the sick and show them that "the kingdom of God has come near you."

## Saving

We need to be a country that inspires saving as much as we do spending. We are great consumers, but we are not great on saving. Then, what we save is taxed so that the incentive "to save" just isn't there.

Rage should be channeled into working with the government and banks into improving the saving of our money for our future.

## Home Buying

Housing restarts have shown us that homes are not of as much value as they were before the Recession. Perhaps it is also a signal that the price for housing is really overpriced.

Affordable housing must come back, and builders (everyone included in the building industry) will be profitable, if they do not overprice a home and undercut on expenses. The greed of the industry has shown itself for what it truly is: greed and overpricing.

## A Few Thoughts on Taxes

Taxes are a necessity to run the country. I remember I was chanting my displeasure over taxes in my young days. A prolific preacher-prophet and pastor, by the name of Nelson H. Smith, Jr. said to me, "the government doesn't stop you from making money, they just say, pay your taxes on it." I hushed to ponder that over the years.

Jesus said give Caesar what is his. That means the tax. However, I am a Democrat, conservative in my Christian beliefs, and moderate in my politics. I believe we should pay a Fair Tax. Some might want to call it a flat tax.

I call it fair in the sense that everyone rich or poor would be paying the same amount of taxes on their income. Savings would not be penalized because a fair tax could be levied in one way that would give American government what it needs to support itself.

Here is where I may be misunderstood, but I hope not. I don't believe we should give government more than we give God. However, I am not in control. But I will share with you what I think will work.

Congress might want to consider this in the very near future, given our failing economy. The answer is not in more taxes; the answer is in fair taxes. What are fair taxes?

The Federal Government would tax us at the cash register, the amount of 10%. Two per cent would go to the States for funding various government ventures. The State, however, could also charge us at the cash register with another 3 %. The County and City could charge us at the cash register one per cent each, for a total fair tax of no more than fifteen cents on the dollar.

That would not only pump money into the economy, it would insure that everyone would pay the same thing: no more and no less. There would be no taxes on our savings or retirement. The Government would get their fair share, be it federal, state, county, or municipal (city), and all would be well. It would also create a moral climate for marriage and family, instead of couples "shacking up" in states that impose a marriage tax.

The IRS would not have to worry about a great deal of paper work on April 15th. That would be eliminated with everything being reported by the merchants. Government would get more because people would feel free to spend more and also to save more. The economy would prosper.

God Almighty only requires ten per cent (Malachi 3:10-12), plus free-will offerings. That would be an equitable equivalent to some degree though debatable, for government. The difference with God and the government is that He promises blessings. The government has a tendency to take more than it gives; this Fair Tax would change this. **The government would prosper and so would America**.

The New Testament passage of Matthew 23:23 should not be forgotten; I mention it again here for reinforcement for addressing social justice issues. Jesus justifies the tithe and adds that social justice issues should not be forsaken, but included with our giving. With the tax, there should still be a government conscience that does right about the poor and the underserved. Government would have more than enough with a fair tax, to "pour out" blessings on the poor. A Fair Tax may not be so bad after all. Thanks for listening.

## Voting

Voting is another area that we must shore up. Voter Registration is mandatory; we must of course promote Voter Education. The Voting Rights Act has been passed.

We must exercise our right to vote. We must not allow fear, intimidation, and apathy to keep us home, or give us an excuse to not vote. It is our Civic duty to elect those we want to represent us. Dr. Joseph E. Lowery, retired President of the Southern Christian Leadership Conference says, "Take your soles (feet) to the polls and vote." That is good for the soul (the person) as well.

Following our conscience and prayerfully voting our convictions will help us tremendously as a people. We show appreciation for our hard won freedoms. Too many people died for us to exercise the right to vote, and then some of us stay home and let the vote go without our input. Our input is important! It may be your vote or mine that swings the election in favor of what is good and acceptable in God's eyes and for the American people. One cannot know, until one casts one's ballot.

It may be our vote that sends a message to a recalcitrant Congress or reluctant State houses, that we don't have to take anything sitting down, and we will not allow you to take our vote for granted. You will never know for sure until you vote.

It may be our vote that inspires the president, in any generation, which the American people want to see things happen that are effective, and show efficiency in how we manage our resources. Our vote is important. We must vote!

Allow me to tell you a personal family story about my great-grandmother, Candus Fikes-Thomas. She went to register to vote in Selma, AL in 1965, after the Voting Rights Bill had become law. Sheriff Jim Clark sent her home with the words, "Candus, there is going to be trouble today. You go on back home so that you won't get hurt." She turned and went home and called my grandmother, Beatrice Clay in Chicago, her daughter, and told her the story. My grandmother asked her, "Momma, what are you going to do?"

She said, "Bea I went home as Sheriff Clarke said. But I am going back tomorrow because 'us gonna' vote." My grandmother told her, "Momma be careful." My grandmother then shared with my grandfather the Rev. K. D. Clay, Sr., and all the family members, "Momma is going to vote." I will never forget that personal, family Civics Lesson. Vote!

This year will signal the revving up of the engines that start with all the hopefuls; who want to be the President of the United States of America. Everyone should say, from this day forward, I'm voting.

I've been voting since I was of age, and never missed a Presidential election. I have learned in my middle and mature years that it is important **NOT** to miss any election!

To miss any election may be fatal to the neighborhood, to the city, to the state and federal government. To miss an election might mean that someone evil slips into office unawares; someone who may take their cue from voter apathy, that no one is watching; that it's time to turn back the clock of progress, back to a time, which no one should want to return. Every election is too important for us not to vote. The Revolutionary War, War of 1812, the Civil War, Women marching for the Right to Vote, African Americans marching for the Right to Vote, are all encouragements to remind us, we must vote.

### Rewarding Innovation

What about making money and rewarding innovation? I have no problem with people making money; that is how America pays her bills when everyone can make money from their gainful employment. There is room, and plenty of it for new innovations; there is always plenty of room for inventing "a better mouse trap."

New innovations need rewarding and should be openly recognized as being something that will enhance our quality of life. But nothing should take place that will be the demise of positive advantages in how we live or need to live. We do not need anything-negative happening at the expense of the American people.
Neither do we need anything happening at the expense of a responsible organization, trying to improve its lot. Lobbying should not cancel our right to advance, in this instance, causing the people you have elected to serve to hinder progress. Lobbying has its advantages and its disadvantages.

### Lobbying

Lobbying should be done with respect and sense of fair play, and what will be good for the American people, not just the special interest groups that stand to benefit from excessiveness gratuity to lawmakers that results in feeding corporate greed.

### Making Needful Changes

We would do well to look at making changes that are helpful. Change, for the sake of good, is the direction we need to move.

Congress needs a fresh objective look at itself. When there is no change, you die. When the government does not look at itself in terms of what is truly needed to succeed, and fails to, in Peter Drucker's words, drop what is no longer essential, it will fail. Drucker's theory that the organization cannot survive on self-centered leadership might be an excellent read for our Congress – Democrats and Republicans and Independents.[42]

Change within the organization and in the American Public Square is in order, rage unchecked and reprogrammed into positive energy for the common good is not healthy. Let's "drop the rage and turn the page" and make America beautiful for all.

---

[42] See Peter F Drucker, *Managing The Non-Profit Organization – Principles and Practices*. (New York: Harper Business, 1990), pp18-27.

# Appendix

## A Sermon Entitled

## "Vote For Jesus For President"

## Preached by the author to the parishioners of the
## Trinity Baptist Church of Metro Atlanta, November 2008

### A Word To My Readers

I am sharing this sermon with you as an extension of my heart. As I mentioned earlier, I recognize that not everyone who reads this book are Christians. Not everyone who reads this book will necessarily become Christian, even though my prayer is that this will change.

What I preached here reflected my own fellowship with the Holy Spirit and a hope that all of the people in our church congregation would think seriously about voting, and the blessing of thinking about what would happen if Jesus were to be president.

I present it here for the same reason, hoping that when you start thinking about who you want in charge of your affairs, the affairs that affect the state of your heart, and that you will cast your vote for Jesus.

The sermon is set up in terms of an explanation of the two passages used from Matthew's gospel account. It transitions into some thoughts about what the subject and message imply. It then moves to what the message is trying to convey in terms of how we apply it to our lives.

It is my hope that it is not overly technical and complicated so that you are burdened by its words, or that it is so simplistic it offers no real challenge to the reader.

Subject: **Vote for Jesus For President**
Matthew 17: 5; 27:21-23

In a presidential election cycle, there will inevitably be people who vote for the wrong candidate because they really don't know the truth about the best candidate. Today, we do not have to make a wrong choice; we can deliberately choose Jesus and vote for Him to be our President for life and for all eternity.

## Explanation

Our two texts convey a message on making the right choice for your leader for all the right reasons, and the folly of choosing the wrong leaders for all the wrong reasons. In both passages the people involved don't know whom they are choosing. In the first passage, they are told who to choose: Jesus. In the second passage, the voices of the people choose someone they know totally nothing about, instead of the One who had done them nothing but good.

In Matthew 17, God steps in and picks His choice to lead His people. Peter has inadvertently blurted out that to honor history they should build three tabernacles: one for Jesus, one for Moses, and one for Elijah, when he and the other two apostles awaken from sleep and see Elijah and Moses talking to Jesus on the Mountain of Transfiguration. His choice had to be overruled by God Himself coming down in a cloud and speaking out on behalf of His Son. "This is My beloved Son, hear Him." To hear Jesus is to make a deliberate choice. In other words, "let Him preside."

In the Matthew 27 passage Pilate is being diplomatic by giving the people the choice as to who should be executed: Jesus the Christ or Barabbas who had committed murder during an insurrection. The multitude made a bad choice because cheap religion was bent on destroying Jesus. A bad mistake to be sure. In choosing Barabbas, they threw away their chance for a true President who would look out for their souls and their welfare. It is necessary that we do not make the same mistake and vote for the devil that will give us nothing but heartbreak. I am on the campaign trail inviting us to see to it that Candidate Jesus gets our vote.

## Implications

In a presidential election Primary in America, the races generally narrow the field down so the best candidate will become the national standard bearer of the leading party in our basically two-party system. This year we are making history because the two-party system has produced a Democratic candidate of color to run against the Republican candidate. We will have to decide which candidate we will vote for. My advice is for you to choose the candidate that best represents your views.

If you do not choose a candidate other people will pick one for you, because they will exercise their right to vote. You must decide today to be an active participant in the voting process. Register, and then vote at election time; every election is important.

When the choices are up to us, we can without apology, decide for ourselves, what we want in a President who will run our country. We look for honesty, integrity; someone who is clear on the issues that dominate the national interests; a well-versed speaker, strong leadership skills, and definitely someone who is concerned about our welfare. The text invites us to see why Jesus makes the best Candidate for President in any election cycle in America or anywhere else around the globe where a nation lays claim to the democratic process. As one of His many spokesmen, I want to present to you Jesus for President!

There are a couple of ground rules. You can't vote unless you have registered. And you cannot stay at the ballot box all day once you have registered. You have to make a choice and then move forward. To register, you must be born again. To vote continuously, you must be part of a local assembly of voting delegates where God is over all and the Holy Spirit is in charge. In the first text (Matthew 17:5) God corrected the people on who He preferred. He campaigned for Jesus!

The people in our second text made a bad choice by rejecting Jesus, voting for the opposition. Those people lived to regret it (27:25). We don't have to repeat their error. When we cast our vote for the Lord Jesus Christ we never have to be ashamed of our choice. Let me share with you why we all should vote for Jesus as President.

Application
I. **Vote for Jesus because He's God's clear choice for leading a world set free** – 17:5.
God has always been clear on whom He wants to lead the free world; by this I mean, a world of people set free from sin. Sometime, as in our text, we want to make choice of others, because we equate them to be, on the same level as Jesus. Peter was about to make this mistake by offering to build booths to commemorate the experience of he, James and John. Peter and the rest had heard about Moses and Elijah, read about them, but he awakens from sleep, and there they are, right before his eyes. The passage does not tell us, how Peter or the others for that fact recognized these spiritual giants of Israel's history, since photography and Videography were not in existence at that time, but they knew these men were.

God intervened to speak because Peter had elevated Moses and Elijah to the same level as Jesus. *"Then answered Peter, and said unto Jesus, 'Lord, it is good for us to be here: if thou wilt, let us make here three tabernacles: one for thee, and one for Moses, and one for Elias.'"* Jesus was whom the prophetic ministries of Moses and Elijah pointed to when they lived on earth.

Moses and Elijah were present to talk to Jesus about His impending death (Luke 9:30-31), not to become equals with Him who is before they were. God had to step in and announce His choice. God the Father's words are direct and understandable, *"This is My beloved Son, in whom I am well pleased; hear ye Him."*

God has more than once stepped in and helped us out of our ignorant choices. The devil has tried to interrupt the current campaign for Christ, each day with insult and innuendo. In some cases it is ever so subtle: you get just so close to voting for Jesus, and then confusion sets in about who is truly the right one. We question the moment with "well, I will take everybody and honor them."

Jesus is the clear choice. He is God's choice for the sinner. He is God's choice for the Church. And He is God's choice for the world. If we are to be free we must **let Him preside;** *"hear Him,"* is what the Scripture invites us to do. Jesus is God's Choice for leading a world set free.

II. **Jesus should be our clear choice over any persons whose intentions are evil** – 27:22
In our second passage it was the custom of the ruling governor to give the people an opportunity to choose whom they wanted freed from the death penalty. This particular year they had two choices before them: one good and one evil. The evil one was chosen because the religious establishment was hell bent on getting Jesus out of the picture. Jesus had challenged their right to serve because of how they treated God, God's house, and others beneath them. For example, they laid aside God's law in favor of their customs. They treated God's house as a house of merchandise when it should have been, correctly, a house of prayer for all nations.

There was separatism and disparity in who worshipped God in freedom and who worshipped God with various distractions such as "selling" in the court of Gentiles at worship time. The Jewish worshippers were favored; the Gentile worshippers lost out; false religion felt Gentiles were beneath the Jews and it was more important for the people of the Law to have no distractions.

With Jesus challenging Jewish theology and practice, they sought to kill him and preferred a murderer to Jesus. Their candidate of choice was Barabbas.

Pilate asked the question about this unusual selection, in chapter 27:22 to give the people a chance to make a better choice because in Pilate's eyes, they made a bad choice. *"What shall I do then with Jesus which is called the Christ? They all say unto him, Let Him be crucified."* In saying so the people cancelled their reservations for heaven (Mk.15:7). The chief priests were evil and promoted clemency for someone whose clear intentions were evil. The chief priest had already made a bad choice before Pilate's question, based on their evil intentions. **We should not be swayed to participate** in voting for someone who is not good for us, and is the choice of those who have evil intentions.

That is why we need to pray to God to help us break free from people and circumstances that are dragging us down. It is the reason why people need to abandon Satan and choose Jesus. The devil is a liar and the father of lies (John 8:44). Jesus will always speak the truth, represent what is good, noble, honest, and is God's ideal. Jesus will free all those who want to be set free from evil. When given the chance, I heartily recommend that we choose Jesus every time. He overcame evil with His good. Jesus defeated the devil on the cross (Col.2: 15), and overcame death and the devil, by rising from the dead, just as He promised. Vote for Jesus! His intentions are always right

III. **Vote for Jesus, because He has the best record on keeping His promises.**
Jesus keeps any promises that He makes. Pilate asked the people who they wanted, and they chose to execute Jesus, not knowing that Jesus had the record of integrity. That is okay. The ruling religious authorities thought to kill Jesus by executing Him on the cross, but He had previously announced *"And I if I be lifted up from the earth, will draw all men unto Me"* (John 12:32). Jesus keeps His promises on forgiveness and pronounced His first Presidential pardon during His heinous execution when a penitent thief wanted to be remembered (Luke 23:34).

His **foreign policy and domestic policy** are closely akin to each other, and have worldwide implications; they are very clear. His ambassadors at home and abroad have His interests at heart. John 10:16 records Jesus' words, *"And other sheep I have which are not of this fold; them also I must bring, and they will hear My voice; and there will be one flock and one shepherd"* (NKJ).

*"But ye shall receive power after that the Holy Ghost is come upon you: and ye shall be witnesses unto me both in Jerusalem, and in all Judaea, and Samaria, and unto the uttermost part of the earth"* (Acts 1:8). Jesus empowers all of those who wish to campaign for Him. All of His party members can recruit without being partisan or prejudicial. Jesus is way to God. He wants everyone to recognize God's plan. Jesus wants the whole world for God or nothing at all.

People are out-of-work and some have gone on welfare through no fault of their own. Jesus is not in favor of keeping people on welfare. He has **a generous welfare to work program** based on faith in what God can do with what you say you really want. *"Therefore, I say unto you, what things soever ye desire, when ye pray, believe that ye receive them, and ye shall have them"* (Mk. 11:24). And to help us believe that we can achieve, He says, *"ask in My name..."* (John 14:13-14).

His **economic stimulus package** is a reciprocal program based on shared responsibility. Listen as Jesus says in Luke 6:38, *"Give, and it will be given to you: good measure, pressed down, shaken together, and running over will be put into your bosom. For with the same measure that you use, it will be measured back to you"* (NKJ) .

Jesus' **universal health care plan comes with encouragement incentives:** (Matthew 11:5) *"The blind receive their sight, and the lame walk, the lepers are cleansed, the deaf hear, the dead are raised up, and the poor have the gospel (good news) preached unto them."* **God knows the poor need some good news.** In His platform Jesus also covers us with information on how He can help us get through the hard times, emotional distresses, worsening circumstances, and tough questions.

In Matthew 11: 28-30 Jesus says, *"Come unto Me, all ye that labor and are heavy laden and I will give you rest"* (KJV).

Jesus wants to bring peace to the whole world. When there is a war, He has never lost a battle, and will win the war, because. He is **the Prince of peace.**

Finally, Jesus is the only one eligible to be our President and our King: "KING OF KINGS AND LORD OF LORDS" (Rev. 19:16). Now that you know all of these things, it's time to make Jesus your Choice. Vote for Jesus for President of your life, forever and ever. He has the best record for keeping His promise all the time. Vote for Jesus for President of your life, forever and ever. Amen.

# Bibliography

ABC News and CNN reported the story

ABC News and World Report on August 20, 2010. You can view the full report and interview that John King had with Reverend Franklin Graham the night before at the CNN and ABC News web pages.

Birch, Bruce C. and Rasmussen, Larry L. *Bible And Ethics In The Christian Life* Minneapolis: Augsburg Publishing House, 1976

Cook, Samuel DuBois., ed. *Benjamin E. Mays, His Life Contributions, and Legacy.* Franklin, TN: Providence House Publishers, 2009.

Christian Broadcasting Network, *700 Club Interview,* October 7, 2010 – viewed and listened to by author.

Gary DeMar, *America's Christian History: The Untold Story.* (Atlanta, GA: American Vision, 1993 and 1995)

Drucker, Peter F., *Managing The Non-Profit Organization – Principles and Practices. New York: Harper Business, 1990.*

Elmore, Charles J., *First Bryan 1788-2001.* Savannah, GA: First Bryan Baptist Church, 2002.

English Dictionary at www.AllWords.com

Fritze, John "Voters Send Angry Messages," in *USA Today November 3, 2010 edition.* McLean, VA.

Genovese, Eugene. *Roll, Jordan, Roll: The World the Slaves Made.* New York, Vintage Books, First Edition,1976. He gives an assessment of the preaching traditions of Prosser, Turner, and Vesey.

Hendricks, Obrey M. *The Politics of Jesus.* New York: Doubleday, 2006.

McMickel, Marvin A. *An Encyclopedia of African American Christian Heritage* Valley Forge: Judson Press, 2002.

Paulson, Ken. Article entitled "Church, State and the First Amendment: What O'Donnell Needs To Know" October 19, 2010, on the First Amendment Center Online web site.

Smith, Jr., T. DeWitt. Sermon: *"Vote For Jesus For President."* Decatur, GA: November 2008.

Taulbert, Clifton. *Eight Habits of the Heart.* New York: Penguin Books, 1997.

Tucker, Cynthia. "Obama's Grand Ol' Misstep," *Atlanta Journal Constitution.* Sunday October 17, 2010.

Underwood, William. BJC Religious Liberty Award Luncheon and Guest Speaker and Recipient, June 25, 2010 in Charlotte, NC. Heard by this writer.

Walker, J. Brent. *Religious Liberty and Church-State Separation.* Brentwood, TN: Baptist History and Heritage Society, 2003.

West, Cornel. *Race Matters.* New York: Vintage Books, A Division of Random House, 1993, 1994.

## A Special Note from Former President Jimmy Carter

To DeWitt: This is a good assessment of the adverse consequences of the sharp partisan divide that is afflicting America. The title of your book really gets to the heart of the matter. I believe it is unprecedented, at least partially caused by the massive influx of money into campaigns, much of it used for negative commercials designed to destroy the character and reputation of opponents. This creates doubt in the minds of voters about the honesty of all candidates, and the animosity carries over to Incumbents' service in public office. This is something that did not exist 25 years ago. With my opponents, Gerald Ford and Ronald Reagan, we referred to each other only as "my distinguished opponent."

Not coincidentally, we also used public funding for our general election campaigns – the $2 per person check-off on income tax returns. Another development, that commenced during my term in office, was the melding of right-wing politics with the Republican Party, with pastors of mega-churches handing out lists of chosen candidates who were for the death penalty, against abortion, for the Gulf War, etc.

This book is a timely warning to America about the dangers of extreme partisanship, which divides our people and impedes the effective conduct of public affairs.

Best wishes, Jimmy Carter

# About The Author

## Dr. T. DeWitt Smith, Jr.

T. DeWitt Smith, Jr., D. Min., was born in Chicago, Il to the late T. DeWitt Smith, Sr. and Ernestine Clay-Smith. He is the eldest son of three children born to this matrimonial union. His early childhood into young adulthood was heavily influenced by his parents, grandparents, and others in the African American Church tradition. He has pastored in Illinois, Ohio, and Georgia for a combination of over forty years.

In this book on religious freedom, race, religion and politics, God and government, he speaks to the issues that seem to torment a restless public, and a political system that seems to be filled with rage that may have more to do with social issues than we have previously admitted to. He challenges his reading audience to honestly examine the rage and unrest with the political system, and turn the page with substantive and positive and productive actions that help transform government into what God intended for it to be: one that serves all Americans without regard to party, race, or religion.

Dr. Smith serves as Senior Pastor of the Trinity Baptist Church of Metro Atlanta in Decatur, GA. From 2006-2010 He served as the 18th President of the Progressive National Baptist Convention, Inc. Along with the four national Baptist and mission presidents, they formed the African American Baptist Collaboration to address social justice issues in Scripture that claim our attention at home and especially in Haiti, America, and other places that have been devastated by storms.

He and his wife are the parents of four children and thirteen grandchildren. He is a graduate of Judson College in Elgin, IL with the B.A degree; and Ashland Theological Seminary in Ashland, OH with the M. Div. and D. Min. degrees. He has authored several church ministry books, and lectures and preaches inside and outside of the America.